Healing and Acceptance

WOMEN LIKE ME

Compiled by Julie Fairhurst

Julie Fairhurst – Rock Star Publishing
Paperback Edition: ISBN 978-1-990639-09-8
Cover Design and Interior Design by STOKE Publishing

At times, some readers may be triggered by a women's story. Should you need to speak with someone, there are many crisis lines, counselors, and doctors that you can reach out to. Find someone that can lend a kind ear to listen to you. That can be a friend, parent, spouse, or anyone you trust. Your local community services may have telephone numbers to assist you.

WOMEN LIKE ME

HEALING AND ACCEPTANCE

JULIE FAIRHURST

ROCK STAR PUBLISHING

CONTENTS

...

"Understanding is the first step to acceptance, and only with acceptance can there be recovery."

J.K. Rowling

INTRODUCTION

We're taught that acceptance is important if you want to get along with people and have good relationships. But are you aware that acceptance is vital to your happiness?

If you're struggling to accept a person or a current/past situation, then you may want to recognize this as a possible 'red flag.' Usually, we are accepting of it all without much stress. However, if you are seriously struggling to accept something, it could be a signal that you have a problem, either in your mindset or your attitude. Are you holding onto a situation? Possibly, your thoughts are too negative, or you are not seeing things clearly.

Regardless of why you may be doing it, if you are doing it, you should get to work to remove the negative mindset that could be holding you back. You will feel so much better about yourself and your life if you work on acceptance.

Now, don't get your back up about what I'm saying here. Acceptance can be similar to forgiveness in terms of someone who hurt you or did you wrong. Forgiveness is not saying it is okay, but it is forgiving so that you can move forward with your life. You are accepting that someone wronged you; that's it. With this realization, it will be easier to leave that past where it belongs behind you.

Acceptance is like that. Your acceptance of your past. You can't change it. You accept it, learn from what happened, and move on. Never stay stuck!

When you live a life of acceptance, you will no longer be spending so much time worrying about your future. You will trust that all things work out for your benefit in the end. You will not be replaying that moment, time, or situation in your past that causes you to relive it over and over. There is nothing worse than waking up one day and finding you have been struck in your past, living the same days, months, and even years over and over again.

There is no ultimate control over others. We live on a planet of eight billion people. Give up the thought of controlling anyone in your life. It's not happening. But you can control yourself and your future. When you accept this and focus on yourself and your path, then healing can begin.

We all need to heal from something in our lives. And depending on where we've been and what we've been through, healing may be a more difficult and longer process than for others. But it must be done. Ask yourself, 'what happens if you don't heal?' Where will you be in a year, five years, or 25 years from now?

We are meant to grow and change in our lives, but we will stay stuck if we are living the same day, month, and year over and over again. The same stressful events and the same negative mindset, and we may not, in the end, have lived a happy and fulfilling life. That would be very sad indeed.

And the healing may not just be for you. Think about the generations to come after you. If you have not done the work with acceptance and healing, you may, by default, pass your story on to your children and grandchildren. Now that would be a shame. And the generational story could continue on and on.

Stand up and say, "no more!" This is what the stories in this book are about. Women who stood up and said, "no more!" And went on to work on healing themselves so that those who come after them can lead a better life. Healing so that they can give their full self to those they love and to the world.

The common theme I hear from the over 70 writers who have written in the Women Like Me book series thus far is, "if I can help just one person, just one family, telling my story will be worth it."

These nine women are accepting their past and healing themselves so that they can be a shining light for others who also need to accept and heal. Some of the stories written in this book are raw and were difficult to get out of their heads and hearts and into the book. But they did it. They did it for themselves, their generations to come, and for you.

We all hope you find acceptance and healing in your life and the lives of your loved ones.

Julie Fairhurst

Founder of Women Like Me

Transformational Story Coach

...

"You couldn't relive your life, skipping the awful parts, without losing what made it worthwhile. You had to accept it as a whole--like the world, or the person you loved."

Stewart O'Nan

PART 1

HEALING AND ACCEPTANCE

"The more you know who you are, and what you want, the less you let things upset you."

Stephanie Perkins

1

A REMEMBERING

MEMORIES CARRIED FROM ONE GENERATION TO THE NEXT

"When She loves, She loves forever."
Mark Anthony

Are the experiences that far off? The memories are carried from one generation and told to the next. Does the passage of time lessen the impact of the experience or memory of the events?

Many stories and experiences have been shared with me over the years. I didn't think much of them until now. Now that I am 50 years old, and my Mom has passed on.

A remembering is what I have left. I hold dear in my heart the memories my Mom, Anne, shared with me. Her childhood and growing up around Sturgeon Lake. I also grew up around Sturgeon Lake and hold my own memories and stories. In the coming paragraphs, I share my Mom Anne Mitchell's account of her experiences and my own experience. Many of these stories are in the very same spaces and places, only many years apart.

A remembering of two young girls one generation apart.

June Palmer – "My Mom Anne was born to Albert and Constance on a cold January night in 1938. The snow was deep, and the winter chill gripped the night – a beautiful girl was born. Albert and Constance had four boys, Norman, Frank, Philip, and Johnny. Their daughters are Bella, Florence, Anne, Margaret, and Marie."

"Dog Eating Prairie is the name of the trap line where Anne was born and grew up until she was about six years old. The family would return for trapping season and live at the homestead during the off-season of trapping."

Anne Mitchell - "I remember when we moved out of the old log house where I was born. We moved into a new cabin; it was not far but in the same area. The old cabin was then used as a shelter for the horses. I remember I was on the roof, and I would throw hay through the hole in the roof for the horses. The only thing left of the old cabin now is the outline. The grass is grown over, and it is hard to tell where the houses were. My Mom used to take care of my grandmother's grave site. It was a simple grave site. A big willow grew out of the middle, and my Mom just kept cleaning around the willow. It was like a grave marker. It is interesting that it grew there. Dog Eaten Prairie was a big field, and then suddenly, this big willow grew on the gravesite and nowhere else."

June Palmer –"Sturgeon Lake, Alberta, is approximately 45 km from Dog Eating Prairie. My mosom (Grandfather) Albert Badger owned land near the Sturgeon Lake Indian Reserve #154. My Mom Anne told me stories of growing up there as a young girl and the chores she had. The area is not far from my Mom's house, along the lake shore of Sturgeon Lake."

Ann Mitchell - "I remember when I had to take the horses down to the lake for water. The trail going down was steep, and I was scared the horses would step on me or run me over. Once down there, I had to use the axe to cut a hole in the ice and dig out the ice chips so the horses could drink."

June Palmer – "Just up the road from my Mom's family homestead is where I grew up. I spent a lot of time playing along the lake shore of Sturgeon Lake. My cousins and I would pick choke cherries along the lake, and then we would have hide and seek wars. Climbing the trees, running up and down the trails along the lake. Swimming at our little swimming spot not far from our house. So many summer days in the water and running in the fields. We loved picking berries and enjoying just being. I drive by these spaces now and remember the fun I had. The realization that those fields were my Mom's horse pasture. Those same berry bushes offered their fruit to my Mom too. The trails up and down to the lake we ran along were the trails my Mom led the horses down to the water!"

Sturgeon Lake Indian Residential School
Calais, Alberta Canada

Also known as St. Francis Xavier Indian Residential School and Calais Indian Residential School. Sturgeon Lake Residential School was operational in Alberta between 1890 and 1961. This school was administered by the Roman Catholic Church and was under the jurisdiction of the Lesser Slave Lake Agency.

Larsson, P. (2013, October 27). Sturgeon Lake Indian Residential School. Retrieved November 9, 2022, from https://eugenicsarchive.ca/discover/institutions/residential/526d5bd

Anne Mitchell – "Saint Francis Xavier Catholic Church is the name of our church at Sturgeon Lake. I attended the Sturgeon Lake Indian Residential School. There were big dormitories with rows on rows of beds. I think there were forty beds on the girl's side. They had the girls and boys on different floors. The older girls were called "charges." They looked after the younger girls. Sometimes those girls were mean."

"The nuns were not nice either. They spoke French, and it was hard to understand them. So, it must have been hard on them too. All the kids spoke Cree, and they spoke French, and it was tough. I think they must have had hard times, also. They must have been sent here. They would say weird words in French. My friend Evelyn and I used to be very close in our school days. The nuns did not like that. They would separate us and say, "Where is your Le Friend now?"

"Now that we are older, that is what we call each other "Le Friend" When Evelyn and I or any of the kids would be playing or holding hands, the nuns would get mad at us and say, "mother cat la!" and pull us apart. That is why I am not comfortable with holding hands or hugs. They made it seem like it was wrong."

"We prayed lots. Early in the morning, we get out of bed and pray on our knees beside our bed. Then we get up and go to the church for morning prayers. We go back to the Mission and have breakfast, pray before breakfast, at lunch, in the evening, and then again at night before bed."

"In the yard, an imaginary line separated the boy's and girl's sides. You got in trouble if you even looked toward the boy's side of the playground. The field to the east of the Mission was full of potatoes. They also had a huge garden. They built a root cellar with five stalls for the potatoes and other root vegetables on either side. That is the place we called spud hill."

June Palmer – "We spent many hours sliding at Spud hill as kids. We didn't have much. It was not like we could go out and buy toboggans or crazy carpets for sliding. We had to make do. I remember this one time we used an old car hood and used it to slide down the hill! There was no such thing as steering on that thing! We also would use cardboard. They do not make cardboard like they used to."

Ann Mitchell - "The priests, brothers, and the nuns had good meals. We kids got what was left. As I got older, I helped in different parts of the Mission. I did lots of sewing, which is where I learned how to sew. I enjoyed it. I can sew pretty good. I used to help out in the kitchen, too, sometimes. We could only go to grade nine, and that was it. After that, you could work at the Mission in the kitchen or elsewhere and make a little money."

"We had some good times. I liked the Christmas concert, this one time I had a guitar that I pretended to play. I am unsure what the play was about, but we had headbands and feathers. I think they dressed us up as Indians! Which is silly. I never did understand that one. I remember hearing the wind whistling through the windows, feeling lonely, and wanting to go home. It was mid-winter; it was so cold outside. I was at the window looking West toward the lake. I saw a long line of army trucks. The old road was part of the old Alaska Highway. They had tanks on trucks and army trucks too."

June Palmar - "I often go to Mission Hill, sit on the guard rails to watch the sunset, and take in the sights of Sturgeon lake. This is called the Mission because the old residential school was nearby.

Not long ago, I was taking in the colors. We have the most amazing, beautiful sunsets here. And then I thought about the children, maybe my Mom and Dad, and how they would have watched the sun go down. But I wondered, did they get to see the beauty of it? Or were they too deep within the sadness and longing to go home to see it? I had an interesting thought as I watched the sun go down. Of all those years my parents were little at that place, did the sunset look the same?"

Anne Mitchell - "I recall getting in trouble this one time, and the nun grabbed me by the back of my arm. They liked pulling you by the ear or pinching the back of your arm and pulling you around. My arm was so sore that I had a big bump, like a blood blister, on the inside of my arm just above the elbow. It was sure painful. I had to stay in the infirmary for a long time. I remember being in so much pain that I could not move my arm or sleep on that side for a long time. To this day, I still have burning pain at times in that arm."

"I recall the underwear inspection that I did not understand. All the girls had to line up and show the nuns both sides. Holding them up high and flip them around and show the other side. If you had an accident or soiled, you were strapped. Lots of stuff happened at the residential school."

June Palmer – "When the school was closed, we used to run around and play in the building. Typical kids playing around. The stairwells and the basement feel exceptionally creepy. I felt the hair on the back of my neck stand on end. I could feel the energy of the spaces. I did not understand empaths or energy readings. This is what I was feeling."

Anne Mitchell - "I remember when we used to help shine the wood floors, we had these chamois on our feet, and we would slide around polishing the hardwood floors of the long hallways. That was kind of fun. You couldn't show you were having too much fun, or you had to do a different job."

June Palmer – "I recall just sitting on the step in the stairwell one day, looking at the crosshatching of the rubber on the kick plates, taking in the detail of the floor tiles in the small rooms. The hardwood flooring just seemed to run on forever with no end. I noticed the baseboards being so tall, about 8 to 10 inches tall. Noticing the dust particles as they floated in the sun beams through the windows. I looked out to the lake and the road, contemplating my next adventure. Maybe go check out the saskatoon berries. They might be ripe. All the time I spent just playing around and did not realize that my Mom and Dad had spent time in these very spaces as kids. Same age as me but in totally different circumstances. They did not see the adventure around every corner. They had a totally different experience than me."

Anne Mitchell - "I loved the Christmas time, midnight mass. I loved the different setups that the nuns did to the altar on different occasions: Easter, Christmas, Lent, and all the different special occasions of the church. I loved the sound of the hymns in Cree. That is why I like to decorate the church for different occasions, especially Christmas. I like making it look nice."

June Palmer - "My Mom spent many hours sewing drapes and different pieces, all color coordinated for the seasons and occasions of the church. My Mom enjoyed making it beautiful for everyone to enjoy. My Mom was a master seamstress and could whip out creations with just a thought. No pattern needed. Just a few measurements and, voila, masterpieces. To this day, they still use my Mom's creations for the church decorations."

"In 2015, my Mom Anne got sick with cancer. We made many trips to Edmonton to specialists and oncologists. It was a very trying time and a whirlwind of a time. On the last trip to Edmonton, the plane was full, and the head nurse told me there was just no room for me to accompany my Mom on this flight. We were sad about it, but Mom was brave and said she would be okay. As luck would have it, on the day of the flight (my birthday), the nurse called me last minute and said there had been a cancelation. They had room for me to attend if I was available! Of course, I jumped at the opportunity. I accompanied my Mom to the Royal Alex hospital for her appointment."

"Once the appointment was finished, we sat outside the hospital, waiting for the ambulance to come and take us back to the airport. Mom and I sat, and we talked about the weather and the city, and she shared with me that it was at this same hospital I spent the first three months of my life in NICU. She talked about how it was so touch and go with my twin brother and me. We were born very early; I was only two pounds four ounces, and my brother Fraser was two pounds eight ounces. She said we were so tiny and our skin seemingly so thin. You could see our little veins etc. We fit in the palm of the nurse's hand; we were so small."

"My brother only lived to be 21 days old. His lungs were not as well developed as mine. I had to stay in the NICU until I reached my scheduled due date, which was in June. Mom said I was about six pounds when she got to take me home. Sitting with my Mom on my 43rd birthday was surreal, talking about labor and the delivery of my brother and me. My Mom was 34 when she had me and my brother Fraser. She had eight little ones at home and was going through all this!"

"Early labor, the loss of a little baby at just 21 days old! Shortly after our delivery, Mom had to go back to the hospital and had surgery for gallstones. It was during the time my Mom was in hospital in Edmonton that my sister Frankie drowned. She was 18 months old. My Mom was such a strong lady. I can not imagine how she made it through so much in such a short time at such a young age. I asked her about it, and she said, "Life goes on."

"I don't know that I could do it. My Mom was a remarkable, strong, resilient, and wise woman. If I can follow in her footsteps and be half the woman she was, I will be blessed.

"My Mom really did love her little church, and we had many talks about how she was baptized at that church. She received communion and married in that little church."

Anne Mitchell - "When the time comes, I want to be brought to the church for evening prayers, viewing, and leave me in state overnight. The next day full mass and funeral."

June Palmer – "When Mom passed in April 2015, I did as she asked and followed her direction to a tee. It was a beautiful mass, and her little church was simply decorated. We chose a lovely set of drapes my Mom had sewn for the altar, and I put red roses about in sparkly vases. Red was Mom's favorite color. My Mom loved her sparkles and sequence materials. She called them sprinkles, as this is what her granddaughters called her sparkly shirts."

"The little church felt so small to me at this moment. I attended church here all my life, many midnight mass with my Mom. I, too, helped decorate for the changing seasons. It never occurred to me that I would one day decorate the little church for my Mom's funeral service. Yet here I was, I fussed over how the drapes hung, positioned the candles just so—made sure the hymn books were in order and double-checked the sound system for the first and second reading. Put out tissue boxes, and triple-check the tea and coffee station. Set out the snacks for the guests. I was constantly rearranging and resetting the drapes at the base of the casket. It looked as though Mom's casket was floating on a cloud. I did an amazing job with the details. Thankful to my sisters and brothers for helping me through and making our Mom's final service a true celebration of her life. My Dad gave me a nod of approval when he arrived and took in the setting of the little church."

"On that last trip home from Edmonton, the weather was exceptionally beautiful, and as luck would have it, we got clearance to land in Valleyview. I shared the news with Mom; she was so relieved and happy, as the ambulance ride from Grande Prairie to Valleyview was so very rough. As we were preparing to land, my Mom shared a story."

Anne Mitchell - "I think I must have been about 11 years old. I ran the horse and wagon, dragging the trees out. My Dad and brothers did the brushing and falling of the trees. Our family did the clearing for the Valleyview airport and the landing strip."

June Palmer - "Wow! Mom, that is crazy. Did you ever think that at 77 years old, you would be landing here?"

"Mom didn't say a word; she just gazed out the window and took in the view as we touched down on the runway. My Mom has a memory of the clearing, and I have a memory of one last plane ride on my birthday with my Mom."

JUNE PALMER

...

"Some people believe holding on and hanging in there
are signs of great strength. However, there are times when it takes
much more strength to know when to let
go and then do it."

Ann Landers

2

FACING ADVERSITIES

I SEE THE LIGHT, AND IT'S BEAUTIFUL

"& to heal you must first allow yourself to feel everything."
/zahra

She was a young girl, too young to know any better and not wanting to see the truth. She just wanted her family, love, and protection and could never understand why her family was so damaged. As she aged and healed, she learned that the only way to gain love and protection was from within oneself.

November 1992, I was born in my hometown of Terrace, British Columbia. I was the third child born into a blended family, my father's first and my mother's third. I was a little sister to my siblings. My father had been raising my siblings with my mother, and soon after I was born, they became pregnant with my little brother, who is thirteen months younger than me.

I want to say that my family was happy and loving, but it wasn't. I believe alcohol played a significant role in my parents' lives. My parents separated when I was around four or five. I was too young to understand why they had separated, but through the separation came grieving, and the little girl I was began to develop behavioral challenges. I just wanted my family together and figured if I acted out, then sure enough, sooner or later, my parents would get back together, but they didn't, and life tended to get seemingly worse as time elapsed.

After my parents' separation, my parental grandmother took my mother to court for her grandparents' rights. I believe my grandmother brought my mother to court because she was controlling, or maybe she cared a little too much. Maybe she had concerns? I am not entirely sure about her reasonings, but my mother became tired of my grandmother's ways and was limiting my grandmother's time spent with us.

I remember mom telling me she would smell my grandmother's perfume in the house when she got home or do constant drives past the house. My grandmother spent a great amount of her life caring for her siblings, so maybe she felt it was her job to be there for her children and grandchildren but in a controlling way. The court granted my grandmother the right to see my little brother and me for two hours once a week. Our time with her was enjoyable at times, but other times not. Most of the time, I figured if I acted out, I wouldn't have to visit, or it would end our visit early.

Thinking back to those weekly visits with my grandmother, we would do things like making unique crafts, but the negatives would overpower the positives. Negative talk about our mother, leaving us in the car with lit cigarettes and the windows rolled up. Telling us how our siblings were not our siblings because they had different fathers. It began to irritate me to the point where I did not want to go there and felt she was cruel for how she spoke to us about my family. It had me puzzled at such a young age. Furthermore, she would take us to the bingo hall where we would either sit in the car or sit in a hotboxed lounge while she set up her evening cards; we could have been at home with our mother as this was not enjoyable for us kids.

My brother and I would go to our dad’s every second weekend, and when we would go to dad's, I would hate it there and just wanted to be back with mom. I felt angry because dad had a girlfriend, and I did not particularly like her. I wished my parents were still together and dad having a girlfriend meant he was moving on from my mom.

Moreover, I did not like how my dad's girlfriend wanted us to call her mom, and that did not sit right with me because I loved my mother and did not want anyone trying to step in place of her. It never seemed like enough time with dad, and when we would go there on Friday, he and his girlfriend would be drinking, and then Saturdays would be a hangover day in bed, usually eating pizza and watching movies. Nonetheless, sometimes we would do activities like crafts, games, or be outdoors. Still, the positive memories are very limited to the adult child I am today, as my memories feel like they are all darkness and negative experiences.

The separation of my parents and the constant battle with my paternal grandmother were only the beginning of my anger through my childhood adversities. As I got older, I noticed this anger coming out whenever someone tried to help me (i.e., school, teachers, peers), and I constantly felt like I was always a problem. I thought that receiving help was a sign of being incompetent and weak. I felt I wasn't good enough because I needed "help."

I remember times in school when I would think my teacher was criticizing my work, and I would get so angry. I remember this one time I was so angry about something that when the principal and another teacher were trying to remove me from the classroom, I began to kick, hit, and bite at them because I was that upset. Another time, a girl said something in class that upset me so much that I took my pencil and stabbed her in the top of her hand. The anger grew, and it grew. I felt alone through elementary school and tried to fit in with the "cool kids." I wanted to feel accepted.

Life passed by so quickly. Looking back on these moments as an adult, I was living in constant chaos. My family found out that my mother had a crack addiction and that she had stored drugs, money, and stolen property at our house. I remember clearly to this day that I went to leave to go hang out with my friends. As I stood looking out our living room window, I saw RCMP walking up towards our house with guns. However, when they noticed me in the window, they returned their weapons to their vehicle.

They came to the door requesting my mother, and from that very moment, everything became blurry. I remember the police requesting that we go into our rooms, and they came to talk to us children separately. Our mother was arrested and taken away in handcuffs. Unsure of what happened to us children, the memories are very faint, but I think I went to stay downstairs with my sister as she had a rental in the same four-plex that our mother rented.

Not long after this incident with the RCMP, our mother's addiction resulted in her leaving us one day while we were at school. It was later found out that she had left us to go to another city, Prince George, to seek treatment as there was nothing in Terrace. It was too hard for her to face us and tell us she was leaving. I'm not 100% sure where I stayed at first, but I do know that I never wanted to live with my father, so I believe that the first of many places I lived with my maternal grandmother.

My mother abandoned us children just before I began grade eight, and I began to spiral downhill. It broke my heart to know that our mother had left her children, and I started smoking cigarettes and marijuana and drinking with new friends. Friends who shared the same interests as me, which allowed me to finally feel as though I was accepted for the girl I was.

While staying with my maternal grandparents, I felt the most connection with my nan as I did with my mother. However, I did not want to listen to my grandparents' rules and had an "I don't give a F**K" attitude that my grandparents would not put up with it, which resulted in consequences, of course.

One evening when my grandparents were heading home from work, they drove past a few kids walking down a dirt road near the train tracks. It was in an industrial area that led us down to the river where we could drink. They saw a few guys carrying a girl out to the road and thought about how the one girl looked like me. They stopped and asked if the girl's name was Katelin, and they gave my grandparents a fake name. My grandparents kept driving past but then turned around because they had a gut feeling it was me. Sure enough, they picked up my young and drunken self.

They then went to our local arena, where my sister had been, at a hockey game because they were so scared for my well-being and did not know what else to do. I was puking blood, and my sister informed them that I probably had alcohol poisoning, so they took me to the hospital, where I had to have my stomach pumped. My blackout was the final push for them, and they called my father to come to get me. When I got to my father's house, I began to disobey the rules because this was not where I wanted to be. I would act out, get into their alcohol and cigarettes, and stay out past curfew.

When I hit grade eight, it wasn't long before I was smoking weed during school hours, ditching classes, and getting into fights; eventually, I got expelled from high school. I figured with being out of school, I would have lots of time to do what I wanted. However, doing what I wanted only got me fighting with family and RCMP involvement. My family decided that I should be placed in foster care.

Things only seemed to get worse for me. I struggled to fit into the foster care homes, I moved around frequently, and the support was limited. When I needed clothing or personal hygiene products, it was never something that they would provide. Eventually, I was placed in one foster care home where the lady would give us twenty dollars and a pack of cigarettes each week for doing our chores. One day something happened, and sure enough, the Ministry of Children and Family Development were looking for a new placement for me. I remember being picked up from my school by the RCMP and taken to the holding cells until they could find a placement for me. It was scary, cold, and lonely.

I also lived with my paternal grandparents throughout the years, but it was so far out of town. It was hard for me to get to town to party, and based on my relationship with my grandmother, it only lasted about a week. I lived with my older sister, but our personalities and addictions always resulted in rivalries.

I was also taken in by my childhood best friend's mother, where this was one of the healthiest and most stable homes I had lived in over the years since my mother abandoned me. Living with my best friend's family allowed me to put myself back into school at an alternate school. I was on the side of the school that supported youth struggling with trauma and complex behavioral needs.

However, I would lose my temper in school, sleep on the couches, and always show up hungover or stoned. Many times, I got suspended, and after a while, I stopped going. Eventually, in 2008, I took off to Drayton Valley, Alberta, to help my sister raise my nephew as she was a single mother.

Living with my sister never lasted very long, and I was now sixteen and left Drayton Valley, Alberta, to live with a guy I knew from my hometown area who had been living in Edmonton. We had been talking before I moved to Drayton Valley and decided to start a relationship. I lived with him and some roommates for almost a year, and eventually, the relationship ended. I ended up back in Terrace, and because of the emotions I was feeling from this transition, I began to party lots with my friend that I was living with at the time.

One day we found a "flap" of cocaine in her bed, and she went to do some, and I said I wanted some. It was so numbing and freeing from the pain I was enduring, but I knew I did not want this life. I knew where it led my mother. I searched for a new place to call home. I went to Abbotsford to live with my family, but after a night while out partying with a family member, I became blacked out drunk. I found myself walking down the dark and lonely Mission/Abbotsford Highway. I was scared and did not know where to go.

An older male stopped and asked me if I was okay and if I needed a ride to town. I was so scared; I did not know what to do and was so afraid that this man could rape and abuse me, but he could also be a protector coming to help me, so I prayed for safety to get me to where I needed to be. I got in the man's truck and was asked where I would like him to drop me off. I did not know where to go, so I asked to be taken to a Tim Horton's, and this is where I contacted a local Woman's Transition House. The shelter was for women and children, but somehow, they were able to get me into the shelter, being seventeen and having nowhere else to turn. I was able to get support to find my own place and began working full-time.

One day while living in Abbotsford, I was offered a job opportunity that I thought would be life-changing. I took the job and was soon headed to a company selling magazine subscriptions traveling through various cities throughout British Columbia and Alberta. The job only lasted two months before a friend told me to get out of it because it was not an income one could live off, nor a lifestyle I wanted to have.

I ended up in Calgary, Alberta, again, living with my sister. As we know how this turns out, I was soon living with a friend. I got a job with her at a sports bar serving. Things seemed to be going right in my life for a short period. However, due to alcohol and drugs, things turned negative, and I was on the run again. Eventually, I ended up back in Terrace. I was finally of legal age in British Columbia and found myself in the local club every weekend, partying and using cocaine excessively. It was then that I became pregnant with my daughter.

I found myself pregnant and alone. Unfortunately, because I had been living an unstable lifestyle for so long and wasn't in a stable relationship, I decided I would forever be a single mother raising my child. I knew that with or without the father involved, I would do what it took to raise my baby and provide her with a good life. I felt the importance of this because it was something that I did not have an opportunity of having. From that moment on, I continued to make small steps to better my life. I worked with what I had and knew at each step of bettering myself so that we could one day have the life I envisioned us having.

When my baby was born, I was blessed with a beautiful daughter who brought pride, joy, and happiness. As time elapsed, I continued to raise my daughter on my own. I had been enrolled in upgrading my education to obtain my BC Adult Graduation Diploma. I had either nursing or social work in mind. I began leaving my daughter with babysitters and found myself drinking and using cocaine once again. I did not like who I was becoming and had to get out of that lifestyle before things worsened.

Once again, I left Terrace. I went to live with my sister in Abbotsford. Living with my sister was another life lesson that reminded me of the lifestyle I did not want for myself and my daughter. Things, as always, did not work out, and I found myself packing our belongings into our car and getting me and my little girl out of that living situation.

We headed to Kelowna to live with a hometown friend; her lifestyle was like my sister's. It was not healthy, and I had to get out, so I took myself and my little girl to a shelter in Kelowna. I felt lost. I did not know where to go. Where to turn to for help. I just knew that I had to protect my little girl.

One day while I was in the Kelowna woman's transition house, I was conversing with an aunt living in Prince George. She said something to me that has forever stuck with me, and it was, "why go back to what you left" and then asked me a question: "why don't you come live in Prince George?" I knew I did not want to make Kelowna my forever home, so I packed our car and headed for Prince George.

At this point, I was tired of the fighting and felt I had nothing left. I could not stay with my aunty as there was no room at her house, so when I arrived in Prince George, I took myself to the woman's shelter for women fleeing abuse. It wasn't the ideal place I would have liked to have been, but it was a safe place that would allow me to get by until I found a place to live.

I arrived in Prince George in the middle of February 2016 and had a job two days after living here and my own place by March. Having an aunt living in Prince George who was living a sober and healthy lifestyle is what I believe inspired me the most to get to where I am today. To begin my recovery and journey to self-discovery.

Initially, I found myself in toxic relationships and involved with the Ministry of Children and Family. I knew that this was not the life I wanted for us, so I told myself that I had to get sober and figure out my life before losing my daughter, which was not what I wanted. Therefore, I worked hard to continue bettering myself.

I began to work at getting sober by stopping partying and doing cocaine, and then quit smoking cigarettes. I went to the College of New Caledonia and applied to get back into upgrading. However, to see where my levels were, I had to complete placement tests. My English was at a grade ten level which meant that I had to do English eleven and twelve, and my Math was at a below-grade eight level which meant that it would take me a long time to get my math up to a grade eleven level.

After completing these courses, I found myself on the college website searching to see if there was a program I could get into without having a grade twelve or math as one of the requirements. It turned out that there were a few that I could take, but the only one that stuck out of interest to me was the social worker university transfer program.

I applied with emotions of fear and self-doubt that ran so freely through my mind. A few months later, I received an acceptance letter. In the fall of 2018, I began the Social Service Worker University Transfer program at the College of New Caledonia. This would allow me the accreditation to enroll in the Bachelor of Social Work at the University of Northern British Columbia in the fall of 2020. I was so excited. I couldn't believe I was going to be fulfilling my dreams. I knew that this would change my life for the better. I was so proud of all I had overcome. To get to this point in my life, taking all the right steps to achieve this with enormous efforts.

I didn't know what to expect, nor did I think about the challenges I would soon face as a single parent attending full-time college courses. However, I felt like I needed to take the recommended number of courses that were on the outline so that I could complete my diploma on time. Nonetheless, at times were probably more than I could handle with minimal support and raising my daughter alone.

Many of my college-level courses were about finding myself and answering questions I had all my life about why I faced the things I faced. It allowed me to begin seeing life differently. It allowed me to gain the knowledge I needed to continue my degree. My main takeaway from starting my educational journey of becoming a social worker is that this is my story, no greater than or less than someone else. However, it is my own. We all have a story, and it doesn’t mean that I should dismiss my story because it’s not as bad as it could have been. We all have a story.

Just as I was beginning to find a sense of self after years of trauma and abandonment, running, and fighting, I was faced with a call home to lay my mother to rest. I had just begun the second semester of my first year and had been enrolled in a course called social work loss and grief. During this course, I would have never thought I would be flying home to say my final goodbyes to my mother.

My mother and I had been working to strengthen our relationship. Still, I carried a lot of resentment and hate towards her for the life I had throughout my adolescence, especially as I faced challenges as an adult. I would take it out on my mother at every challenge I faced in my adulthood before she passed, as if it was all her fault.

While spending the final hours with my mother, I told her how beautiful she was and how much I loved her. I thanked my mother for the life she gave me and for the woman I was becoming. I thanked her for giving me the strength never to give up and told her how she gave all her children the strength to fight through life, just like she had. She fought like hell to try and get out of her addictions. She always wanted to do better than she was doing.

However, I believe the addiction was stronger than her, and years of active addiction resulted in her body deteriorating and, eventually, her organs shut down. I sang to my mother and took pictures with her that I will cherish forever. I prayed for God to bring her home peacefully, freeing her of all her pain, and thanked him for taking her home so that she no longer suffers.

While singing to my mother, I watched a tear roll down her cheek. I watched her beautiful facial features so closely that, at one point, it looked like my mother smiled to respond to what I was saying. I remember her beautiful, freshly painted red sparkly nails. I couldn't leave her side and was the last to leave the room after the doctor had stopped her life support. Oh, what I would have done to have changed the way she lived her life so that she would have been in our lives longer. Nonetheless, I know that she is what keeps me going through all the barriers that I have faced and will continue to face. I can heal and no longer resent or present hate towards my mother.

While completing my diploma at the College, I volunteered at the Salvation Army food bank. Volunteering was a requirement to get into my diploma program, and the Salvation Army was one of the places I chose. I continued volunteering once a week while studying, which brought me pride and joy.

I also utilized the services as a single mother on student loans, and attending full-time studies made it harder to gain extra income to live and support myself and my daughter. I utilized the services as much as possible by accessing the food bank twice a week and applying for the Christmas hampers. I did this to help me and my daughter, so during my breaks between classes, I would go to the food bank, as it was across the street from the College, and get my food hampers.

While completing my diploma at the College, I had the opportunity to share my story through the College of New Caledonia and Salvation Army. I was absolutely honored that two entities within the community wanted to hear more about my story and share it publicly. At the end of my education to receive my diploma, I took total control of my health and well-being and my daughter's health and well-being. I began making healthier choices with my diet and exercising regularly.

These things allowed me to work further at my healing. Due to the Covid pandemic, being isolated at home with a child and no support, I didn't believe that I was going to complete my education. It was shocking to change the way of learning. It was so hard attending school with a child at home needing my 24/7 attention. My instructors were understanding and compassionate about the pandemic and worked with their students to ensure they would not fail. Throughout my degree, online learning made my ability to learn more challenging, but I am proud to say that I DID IT. Through each challenge I faced, I kept going because I knew the ending would be so worth it.

After completing my degree, I struggled to get a social work position. I was in full-on survival mode and had no money left from student loans. I had been applying for jobs while still in school and figured I would have landed a job so I could start right when I was done. I did not plan out the financials for when I finished school and had no other source of income to fall back on. I believed that I lacked confidence and felt like I was competing against everyone I went to school with in every interview I attended.

However, I was only competing against myself and probably could have done a lot more to set myself up for success. However, being in survival mode with high-stress levels made it difficult. I hadn't worked for four years. Being isolated from my peers during my degree has also played a huge part in my inability to articulate my skills effectively during those interviews.

Finally, after about a month of no luck finding a job, I had to again apply for welfare. I had to jump through hoops and be on an employment search plan, where they referred me to WorkBC. I was made aware that I needed to work on building up my skills to allow me to become a successful candidate in my interviewing process. I had to learn how to prepare for panel interviews by learning the different behavioral and competency-based questions

I would be asked. I had no idea that completing a degree would mean I would still have so much work to do before becoming a professional social worker.

Eventually, I got a part-time job as a therapy assistant, but it would only provide me with a maximum of three hours a week, so I began applying for jobs again. I was able to obtain full-time employment as an outreach worker. I was so excited because I knew both jobs would allow me to build up my professional development by serving and supporting those living with mental health concerns and addictions.

During my work searching, my relative shared about a book she wrote in and shared with me about joining the Women Like Me Community. I loved the community and books that I had purchased, so I began writing in the women like me community books. Writing has allowed me to work further at my healing and self-care. It allows me to clear my mind. It allows me to value myself and see my worth. I can let go of my fears and be vulnerable by sharing my story.

I began to share my story, hoping that someone out there finds it and uses it as a survival guide to help them overcome their fears and doubts. I began working towards empowering women by sharing my story through different methods (social media, talking to women, sharing through services in the community, or in any way that I could). I can finally see the light at the end of the long dark tunnel I walked through for years. I am working on releasing all the built-up anger and anxiety within me, one day at a time. I am beginning to shed my past and make room for my new life. I am holding the hand of the child within me and reliving my childhood through my parenting. I am proud of myself and can finally see my self-worth for the woman I am.

A final piece I would like to tell my readers is to always believe in yourself. No matter the struggle you will walk, if you believe in yourself, you will achieve great things. Facing adversities led me to obtain great strength, empathy, and compassion. I am on a new journey to self-discovery. I aim to empower others, for I know how hard it is to struggle mentally, physically, and emotionally but financially—all while wanting out of the hard times rather than being patient with the process of life. I feel myself slowly coming out of a dark tunnel. I can see the light at the end, and it is beautiful to look at my transformation and tell myself that I am proud of never giving up on my dreams.

I believe that if someone like myself can overcome adversities, I know you can too. But only if you believe in yourself the way I believe in you.

KATELIN STANVICK

...

"Every woman that finally figured out her worth, has picked up her suitcases of pride and boarded a flight to freedom, which landed in the valley of change."

Shannon L. Alder

3

UN-APOLOGETICALLY ME

LIVING WITH ADHD

"Although the world is full of suffering, it is also full of the overcoming of it." Helen Keller

Imagine you have a minute to win it and are standing in one of those clear shower-looking compartments you see on game shows where they turn on the wind, money flies all around you, and your job is to catch as much of it as you can and stuff it into your pockets, pants, bra or wherever you can put some.

Imagine this money is your thoughts, and this room is your brain. Imagine if there is no off button. This is exactly how my mind works. Always on, always fast, very messy, and it's harder than hell to catch much of anything.

My 20-year-old self was full of zest with boundless energy. I was also beyond frustrated and depressed. I just couldn't think straight. I was going around in circles. I had the attention span of a goldfish and rocket fuel in my veins. Was I just stupid? Was I crazy, or did I have a brain tumor? My mind runs away with me sometimes.

Simple answer - No.

Doc looked me straight in the eye and says – You are not only *not* crazy; you are not lazy, and you do not likely have a brain tumor. You will be OK.

I fell in love with this old doc, soft-spoken English gentleman in the white coat and stethoscope hanging from his neck. That 60 - minutes changed my life and my overall view of myself. It gave me hope again, which gave me a little more control over my run-a-way brain. I was not all those things I thought of myself. My attitude shifted just by knowing that I was not stupid.

Despite my "circuit stances," this diagnosis gave me my *life back,* and it now gives me a purpose to share what I have learned.

"What the hell is my problem?" I asked him. Turns out, I have some different *wiring connections* up there in the old *central command center,* but in the whole scheme of things, I will be OK. I will cope. Now that I knew what I was dealing with, I could accept the challenge and get on with life.

Luckily, I felt *fairly confident,* thanks in part to my speedy processor. No time for wallowing in self-pity. I had excitement bubbling up in me, and I felt emotional. I remember having a cry after that meeting – which I do not do often, but they were tears of joy. But I did not share my tears or my fears with anyone. I just felt the relief of just knowing.

Even though I felt better temporarily, I was still ashamed of myself because I had this thing that was hard to explain. I am not sure if deficit is the right way to describe it, but if so, this deficit is invisible to the naked eye, so relationships sometimes start strong until they catch on, if you know what I mean.

I do not look any different than others, but until I feel understood and accepted by someone, I am awkward as f**k in so many ways. It is not an ideal situation, but on the bright side, there are far worse things in the deficit department if you ask me.

Thirty - five years ago, it was not a thing people talked much about, and to this day, it still does not have an "awareness day" in the calendar that I am aware of. For such a big problem, in my opinion, it was not a common diagnosis. It was scrutinized and ridiculed by some, and then a few short years later, every kid in school that had energy and a naughty side was lining up to be labeled with it.

The flip-flop seemed to cripple its credibility somehow. If you haven't figured me out yet, I am referring to Attention Deficit Disorder. (ADD) or ADHD attention deficit AND Hyperactivity in many of us. Think about it, the deficit of attention plus hyperactivity. Meaning no focus and rushing everything and everywhere. How frustrating is life when you lack things as important as this? EXTREMELY frustrating. It is a very real issue; I can personally attest to it, and I can now spot a member of my tribe a mile away.

I would imagine the human brain and neurological disorders are the body's greatest mystery. There are so many "letters" or acronyms to describe and label our conditions or disorders. Is normal (whatever that is) NRML? I must admit that would be funny. I have never seen it on the list, so I guess there is no such thing. It is not that I dwell on or compare peoples' letters, but if I had an OCD (obsessive-compulsive disorder), for example, such as cleaning OCD or organizing OCD, I think would be much happier with that, despite the that it has its own set of limitations in life. Point is, we all have some letters, and we just must make the best of it.

As a young woman entering adulthood, I had this zest for life. I felt like I could take on the world! I cannot help but wonder if I have a touch of bipolar on top of it. I am high on life. Fortunately, not so many lows in my world. Occasionally, when I had a slower-than-normal moment (when I was hungover or very tired), I have sobering thoughts and think to myself, I am a lot of work. Who will want me? And if I manage to find a good one and hide it for some time, will they keep me?

I have been told a time or two that I am enjoyable in small doses. Well, that one hurts a bit, but it is what it is. I feel the same way about others from time to time.

Feeling rushed is very typical, and I am not a very good listener because I fade out and into my own thoughts. I also constantly interrupt others – unintentionally, of course - and if I am around my people or I am excited about something, I talk way more than my share. My mouth flies open at will, and my thoughts exit randomly and often. But to put those thoughts and ideas into action or motion, well, it is not an easy task. I am sure I am not taken all that seriously when I speak about my lofty goals and dreams. I have literally witnessed people's jaw drop at the things that escaped my mouth without warning.

I have so much to say, and I have so many questions. I have an inquisitive mind. Many people, like me, get so excited sometimes it can be difficult to explain our thoughts intelligently or take logical chronological steps. I must remind myself to stop, breathe and think this through a little bit before I act on whatever mind-blowing idea strikes me.

After 34 years of practice, I recognize my limitations now, so I know I what I can and cannot do well. I can outsource what I need to.

If you only knew how long it took me to realize I can only wear a 1-inch heel, for example. The seemingly simple act of paying attention to what works well and feels right goes a long way. I bought the wrong shoes for 30+ years. Then it finally dawned on me what the problem was!

It was not easy being me at 20, and it still is not today. Obviously, as a young person, you have fewer responsibilities, so there was less pressure. My thoughts are still fleeting, so combining that with the natural progression of forgetting things, it is harder in certain ways.

And adulting creates way more pressure to have your proverbial shit together. I hide things from myself without thinking – I simply don't pay attention to where I am putting something down. My world is full of hide and seek, lost, and found, here today and gone tomorrow. These are all symptoms of my mindlessness.

As with money, I have made great money all my working life, but I did not pay attention to what I was doing with it. Now that my working life is almost over and I do not have much in the way of savings, I suffer from the occasional bout of panic when thinking about it. All I can do now is just carry on, probably working till I am dead and trusting that all will work out OK.

What is the cause of this disorder? I wish I knew, but I don't have the time to research it. I have noticed that this appears to run in families. My child and his father also suffer this fate. Think about that, two parents with messy, disorganized brains trying to raise an equally hell-raising hyperactive child. We were a real package.

No one was ever really in control of the situation for the first seven or eight years. Once my son was old enough to talk to and reason with, things got easier. I also met a wonderful man that balanced my crazy with his calm.

I felt the burden of so much responsibility, and parenting was hard. I worried about his fearlessness day and night and that he would hurt himself somehow. Most parents would just savor those young years. Enjoying their babies, but I wanted mine to grow up fast, so I could talk to him about him, to warn him about himself if that makes any sense. If I could get him to understand himself sooner than I understood *myself,* he would benefit from that.

Knowledge is power, I have always believed. This kid was a handful of all things good and kind and funny. Luckily, he is blessed with a sunny personality because I could not keep him clean, or his things organized. We were a messy bunch, but he was well taken care of.

It was typical that I would lose the school notices or his homework, forget to send permission slips back, and forget the gym strip. I felt like a lousy parent and avoided all interaction at school or helping at PAC clubs. I also avoided talking about this on behalf of myself or my child with others or teachers for fear of exposing myself. I was not strong enough or brave enough to say – This is our situation; extra help is required, and patience is appreciated. I was just too busy managing our messy lives for parent-teacher interviews.

Occasionally I would get brave and feel motivated to talk about it, but for many people like me, communicating intelligently is the biggest challenge. He was guilty of clowning around in class more often than sitting quietly and working, which was his nature. He had the report cards saying he could do better if he would apply himself. I had those same report cards. I desperately wanted to express that if he had trouble getting it, it was not because he was lazy or did not try. His disruptive behavior was a side effect of the wiring problem. I wanted to explain, but because having to explain something I did not fully understand myself, I felt like I was offering up excuses. I hate the word excuse.

Ironically, he being a kid, and his disorganization stemmed from my lack of disorganization. How could I possibly teach him something I cannot do well, either? Suffice it to say; I was not much help in the homework department if we managed to take it home at all, seeing as I could not keep my own shit together. While juggling life, making money, and raising a going concern, it is a detail of least importance when the kids are young. Getting my kid's lunch ready every day was hard enough.

More importantly, as he grew older and wiser, I did my best to educate him to understand himself and be proud of himself just as he is. Despite having this challenge, he is super smart, super motivated, and has definite gifts. Now, as an adult, he is thriving and goes through life with confidence. He has strengths and weaknesses just like everyone else. But he also has superpowers. He knows who he is and what he excels at, and I am very proud of him.

These days, I do not obsess about what other people think about me, but my hope is to educate others where I see an opportunity. It might help someone else feel better about themselves and to know they, too, have a massive tribe out there with unique and wonderful superpowers such as energy, fearlessness, exuberance, and confidence to achieve their wildest dreams.

Performance Anxiety was my side effect. We all suffer from inferiority and self-doubt from time to time. I've always struggled with fairly debilitating performance anxiety, and I feared being scrutinized by bosses or peers. I would easily get jobs but move on quickly. Maybe it was in part self-preservation as I did not think myself worthy of an organization long term.

I also felt workplaces were very cliquey and that I did not fit in for some reason. I was neither interested in politics or drama nor having to impress people, even though I wanted everyone to like me. I chose jobs where I did not have someone looking over my shoulder and avoided jobs where I had to work in teams. I still, to this day, much prefer the solo gig. The downside is that it is a little lonely during the workday, but my customers are my human connection.

I also did not want to work for someone who could fire me. This is a very real fear stemming from being fired twice in my early working years due to my inattention and hyperactivity. Boredom is also a major thing. I need a challenge so challenging, I would find.

Even today, being self-employed, I tend to choose short-term relationships. Anyone can squeak by for the short term. I had this notion that once they figured out something was up, I was a goner or would not be asked back. Because of this and my lack of organization and attention to detail, I never fostered ongoing relationships with clients. I was afraid to reach out after the fact for fear I may be disturbing them, or maybe they did not like me that much to begin with, and I felt uncomfortable asking for the business. Or I might have done something wrong in the past, and I certainly did not think I could handle that feedback.

In my own mind, it was probably bad. Though I am sure now, it was all good, but our thoughts and self-talk can be our worst enemy. Now I choose to look at the positive, wearing those rose-colored sunglasses because my future is so bright.

My aha moment came to be when I was about 20 when I read an article in a Chatelaine Magazine about this woman who would do endless laps around her house all day long trying to get her chores done. She was going steady but never truly finished anything by the end of the day. Her husband would come home after work and bitch at her for being lazy and watching TV all day long.

This wasn't true. She was always in motion, always doing something (including making new messes along the way), yet always trying her best to tidy up, organize and conquer her chores list. She would do a little bit of this and that in an attempt to get everything done. She was a mega multi-tasker (which I used to brag about on my resume). The art of doing more than one thing at a time, right?

In actuality, she was going in circles without ever fully completing a task. It was exhausting. She fell into bed every night, feeling unaccomplished and frustrated. The article then went on to explain that she may have ADHD and what the symptoms were. That was my "AHA" moment. This was me to a T.

I eventually came to realize that people like me live in this wind tunnel of thoughts and emotions that zoom around in our heads so fast that we cannot act on them before they are replaced with new ones or process them in a step-by-step kind of way.

I still and always will do endless laps all day long. I go back and forth down my hallway so many times I am wearing a path in the hardwood. I have a lot of "forgot my thought in transit issues," so I go back to the thought-of-it-spot. I really do have the attention span of a goldfish. I am easily distracted. Oh, so many shiny things. So much to do and so little time. So, I do it in fits and spurts, or laps, some might say.

I put some clothes in the laundry, but I walk away without starting it because I realized I should throw tea towels in, only ending up in the kitchen where the chaos lives, thinking I need to get started on the dishes so I would turn on the water add soap and walk away for just a sec to check my email, end up paying some bills, while letting the sink overrun onto the floor, so now I have to mop up the floor, while getting the mop I start the laundry without the tea towels and decide to quickly change the rank smelling cat box, and feed the dogs while I am at it. Luckily, I have bomb-proof linoleum flooring.

I am sure it sounds amusing. But let me assure you that this comedy of errors is extremely time-consuming and aggravating. If you had any idea how many times the t-shirt goes back in the dryer with the fresh wash to unwrinkle it because it never gets hung up quickly, you would be shocked.

Even though I have personally come to terms with myself, some folks might consider this diagnosis to be a cop-out on being responsible for life's messes. They may think it is all about choices. You can choose to be more organized, for example.

Sure, life is about choices, but if I had a choice, believe you me, I would not be living in this damn wind tunnel. It is like nothing has time to stick or sink in. I'm always feeling late for something and in a constant state of indecision and flux. If only I could turn it off and form control over my thoughts, words, and emotions, I would take baby steps instead of skipping steps. I would know what I want and how to go get it. I would put the horse before the cart and one foot in front of the other. I would get there slowly and steadily. I often wonder how successful I would be if only I did not have this messy brain to deal with.

Piles and files. I do not know about you, but I like to see my "things" I feel like I am more organized if I can see them. Even though I cannot really see them since they are in piles, I repeatedly shuffle through my piles and files and take mental notes as I have a good visual memory. Zero auditory memory and mediocre tactile memory. Where did I put that?

I am sure I have at least three of everything. I used to also buy new gadgets and organizational junk that just ends up in a corner hiding my junk. Organization is not my strong suit, so I am always looking for ways to organize myself.

Open cabinet doors are one of those pet peeves my hubby gets annoyed about. If you can open it, why can you not close it? That is a fair question. People like me have trouble sorting things also. Socks are my nightmare, as they never go to the laundry together. Not all things have a place in my world, such as bits of paper. What the hell am I going to do with all this paper? I do have a very hard time shredding as what if I shred the wrong thing, and who's got time for that? I might not be able to find it, but at least I did not shred it. As for clothes, shoes, and Halloween costumes from years gone by, I keep them well past their overdue date. I may fit into that someday, right?

Decisions and more decisions. What to do with this or that homeless item? Some days that just stymies me. When I do purge stuff, I give everything away to charities supporting the less fortunate. I believe many homeless people suffer from ADD, probably combined with other neurological disorders. They are on the street for many reasons and personal circumstances, but one thing is for sure, through no fault of their own, if they suffer from this, they are poor decision-makers, have trouble sorting out and working through the details, and keeping their proverbial shit together.

Sufferers commonly have very low self-esteem and are so reliant on whatever vice helps them to slow down their messy brains the escapism debilitates them further until they cannot really function amongst the general population. I am sure they feel less than and hopeless about change. This is a sad fact. It is not recognized for the debilitating thing that it is and therefore is no real support groups to lean on. I often wonder what I could do about that.

Now in my fifties, I am naturally slower. I still misfire in the old command center but moving at a slower pace, so there is less financial carnage. I plain old have less energy to start new things, and I am hopeful for a simpler life. I occasionally still get excited about new adventures and am glad to be amongst the land of the living. I still have bouts of endless energy, and I always need something to do, but it's not the crazy train I once lived.

Financial carnage is a real side effect. Unfortunately, more so since the age of the internet, I have wasted thousands online. It is so easy to sign up for this or buy into that expensive course online that will fix me, make me money, help me lose weight, or whatever. It is kind of like a gambling addiction, I would think. I used to shop therapy myself broke, wearing only a quarter of my wardrobe ever and plain old wasting resources. I buy things I think I need and rarely take them back because I lose receipts so easily. It is in that pile of paper somewhere, but who has that kind of time to look? Easy-to-follow systems would help, but I need help creating them. Does anyone want to collaborate?

People like me could also really benefit from a financial planner or, at the very least, an advisor or ADHD coach to help steer us away from instant gratification scenarios. FOMO - Fear of missing out is a real fear. I have been known to be whimsical and impulsive, and I often cannot think far enough ahead to realize the potential consequences of my spending actions. That is why I am where I am today. Not yet rich.

Dragons Den is one of my favorite shows, and I get so much inspiration there. Sometimes when I think up that next big thing, I feel as if I had won the lottery. I get so excited because I think big. Really BIG. Until a week in or so, I lose interest because 1) I do not have the natural ability to run a scalable business. 2) I do not know how to go about impressing people that know the business and are willing to team up 3) I have no disposable income.

Over the years, I have wasted so much money on starting up this or that half-assed project and going nowhere fast. People with a correctly wired command center naturally do better in life because they can comprehend and complete. People like me fly by the seat of our pants, engaging in new things regularly to entertain themselves, it seems.

So much to do. So little time. I do have brief moments of focus, but they are fleeting. I lack patience and persistence. Time blows by at warp speed, and I feel like there is never enough TIME to put that thing back in its place or file that piece of paper right now or look at my bills and bank statements or start that book I want to read. Time is an extra precious commodity for us who must do several loop arounds to get our to-do lists done. What is time management anyway? As in writing this chapter, I've gone over it hundreds of times to add/delete and edit. It was probably fine after the fourth review, but here I plunk away at the computer while my bathtub almost overflows. True story just now. (I just caught it just in time)

I should be doing something that needs doing, such as paying bills, cleaning the house, and organizing something with every spare minute I have. I am a procrastinator if I have something uncomfortable or scary to do, like handing over money. I always worry about not having enough.

I also recognize that I have a limited emotional range. I have stifled my voice and stuffed down my feelings because I did not know how to express them. I refuse to be vulnerable. When asked the age-old question of what is wrong. I just shut down. When pressed, getting the point out takes some time. I am like an onion that needs peeling. Gently. Also, I shed very few tears, even when I need a good cry. And believe me, I need a few hundred good cries.

Communication is a tool in my toolbox that needs sharpening. People like me sometimes appear to be accusatory, disingenuous, or passive-aggressive when trying to get our point across. I am admittedly a lousy communicator – when I am excited about something, words come flying out in a swoosh of mumbling gibberish. I must sort my thoughts on the fly- so I am always afraid of what I will say. I often say too much (much like the person who cannot tell a lie), or it comes out all wrong, or I clam right up and say nothing at all. I try to be witty, for I feel that sometimes I have nothing intelligent to say.

In my younger days, I was busy trying to be liked, cool and fun. For lack of any identifiable skill set, I joined in the pot smokers club early on in high school because I was struggling in school. I could memorize, but I just could not piece together or figure out many things academics required. I believe this club was made up of mostly people like myself. People trying to slow the hurricane in their heads and catch some of those fleeting thoughts. Marijuana was probably my saving grace. Now that it is legal and comes in many useful, socially acceptable forms, I do not have to be ashamed of using it. It brings me to a place of calm and focus. I get the tedious done in that state of mind.

People may assume that if you have ADHD, you cannot focus on *anything* without being medicated. If that were true, it would be dangerous to roam the earth. Let me assure you. It is not quite that serious. Pressure and deadlines actually help. It is a weird side effect. Our basic common sense is still intact and fine-tuned when obvious danger is present. Some peoples' version of danger is different from others, and I have done bold and silly things like trying to get that perfect up-close shot of the rattlesnake ready to strike or riding my motorcycle too fast.

People like me tend to have an invincibility quality – it will never happen to me - and lack a certain amount of foresight at times. There is a certain level of "must be extra careful" and attentive when crossing the street if distracted or getting behind the wheel when you are just learning. Autopilot is dangerous.

My life was saved crossing the street one day. I had to be yanked out of the path of a moving vehicle, and I was nearly hit. This was a yield situation where the car was supposed to yield to me when entering the crosswalk; however, I did not look, and it did not either. My hubby jokes I only have one speed, and that is GO- Problem is that I go full tilt. I was in go mode that day. Day in and day out, I practically run everywhere I go (speed-walking) and do not have a leisurely setting. But that day my guy saved me from being run down was a wake-up call. Sure, I have suffered other self-induced maladies, but now, I am more conscientious about what I am doing. I practice the art of look before I leap and shoulder check before I turn or stand up because aside from almost being run over, I cannot count the times I left a cupboard door open, stood up fast, and whacked myself a good one.

People like me have superpowers too. When doing something we enjoy, we hyper-focus and achieve excellence at our undertakings. As with anybody, when we love what we do, we do it well. When we love what we are learning, we learn it well. I love driving, and I love teaching, so according to the feedback, I am an excellent driving teacher, and believe it or not, I am super focused in the car.

I missed a few boats along the way, for sure. I have thought up a few businesses that came to be, except that I didn't bring them to fruition. Someone else started booster juice. Back in the 80s, before fast food smoothies were a thing, I thought that juice & java junction drive-throughs would make a great business and look at them today.

I consider my superpowers to be forward-thinking paired with blind faith and fearlessness to blaze new trails that I know nothing about. Some might call this stupidity. I am willing to learn, and if I fall, I just get right back up and keep going. I have unwavering faith in myself. Yes, it takes longer to get my ass back up off the ground, but I am always in motion. Always moving forward, hardly looking back, and never really looking within. I am honestly a little bit afraid of what is in there deep down.

I knew I was different, but I still cannot figure out why I have always felt like an imposter in a world of fearless high achievers. I am also fearless and a high achiever in many respects. I have done well, but if I could go back, I would change a few things. I would have gotten medicated at an early age before the self-medicating started.

For many years, I have self-medicated and abused my body and my soul with smoking, drinking, and food. I still struggle with smoking, drinking, and food, and I often think, why am I slowly killing myself? I am a good human, and I do not deserve self-sabotage.

Well, I admit, on occasion, I think about once life here on earth is over, whenever that may be, how much easier it would be on the other side. Floating around as an orb-like, I see in almost all my pictures. Haunting those I care about gently, like my printer that runs on for no reason just about every day or the apparitions I think I catch a glimpse of out of the corner of my eye. What is it like up there? Carefree, just being social with other orb floaties.

Even though life is challenging and scary, I do not want to die young, especially by my own hand, at least not until I have lived what I consider to be a purpose-filled life. I have lived on the edge many a time, yet I must have a bigger purpose because I am still here. I must still have work to do and my voice to use.

Despite having some difficulty in communicating "on the fly," I have finally found my voice, and these days, not only do I stand up for myself, but I will actively engage in protest and debate.

In this new world of do what you're told or else, something has lit a fire within me to use my voice for good. I do not cower from conflict like I used to. I encourage you to do the same. Speaking up for yourself is cleansing.

In our world today, I can hardly believe what I am hearing, and it seems we have gone back in time to a place I don't want to be. We are living in a bad dream. Political correctness be damned. I actively seek out alternative thinkers and media sources for clarity and balance. I no longer believe everything I see or hear. I am now a critical thinker, and I am very afraid of what is in store for us.

This world is making me increasingly angry. I feel wronged in so many ways. Response is difficult in part because I could never communicate my feelings in a clear way before writing. I can hardly say, "hold that thought, buddy, while I write you a response," ha-ha.

For someone who has a hard time keeping thoughts in my head, I am also a grudge holder. I harbor hard feelings easily, and forgiveness is not my strong suit. I really struggle with forgiving those who have hurt me or hurt those I love. I know I need to stop obsessing, even hating, I am ashamed to say, and wishing ill will. Hate is a terrible emotion, and sometimes I think if only I had a voodoo doll, that could be so healing! The thought has crossed my mind.

The reality is that I take little comfort in the fact that I could never be that person that hurts others for the satisfaction of it. I am bitter and angry that there are people in this world that only serve themselves and purposely hurt others for no good reason just because they can. I hang on to the notion that they must feel less than themselves, and usually, the bully is also hurting. I am working on forgiving myself for my nasty thoughts and forgiving them for their nasty actions. I trust that Karma will take care of it, so I will do some good in this world to make up for the awful people out there roaming the earth, still living and breathing. Why do only the good die young? I have never understood.

Just like everyone else in this world, I have suffered great losses. I have lost friends, cousins, my father, brother, stepfather, and father-in-law. Yet I do not know how to grieve, and I do not like going within to feel and process loss. I am an avoider of all things emotional, and I tend to bury such feelings. I am a very surface-level human, it seems, even though I hurt just like everyone else. I hate the taste of tears, and I avoid that at all costs.

For those of you who may think I still need to get my shit together. I can only remind you that I proudly have rocket fuel in my veins. And my shit is as together as it will ever be. Xo

This deficit has no cure, only management. There are plenty of pharmaceuticals to choose from, but I prefer good old-fashioned marijuana products such as CBD oil and mental calm vitamins. Meditation sessions are great for practicing getting out of your head and resting your body mid-day.

My wish for you is that you find your voice, embrace your superpowers, and know that you are unique and special too. And just be a good human.

LISA KALINSKI

Hot Tip

I found an amazing website called Attitude, and they publish a really good magazine also. They are a source of positivity and a wealth of productivity tips.

ADDitude - ADD & ADHD Symptom Tests, Signs, Treatment, Support (additudemag.com)

...

"Sometimes people let the same problem make them miserable for years when they could just say, *So what.* That's one of my favorite things to say. *So what.*"

Andy Warhol

4

A BROKEN MIND

OUR JOURNEY WITH SEVERE MENTAL ILLNESS

"I have learned now that while those who speak about one's miseries usually hurt, those who keep silence hurt more.'
C.S. Lewis

At 3 am, the nurse comes by and tells us we should go home and get some rest. They have him and will take good care of him. We look at her, at each other, and back at her. "No way, I can't leave him. I won't leave him," I say. We find a place to try to rest, and we wait for morning and hopefully a bed in the Psych ward. I've never been in a Psych ward before, and we have no idea what to expect. How did we get here?

High school was tough. Like really tough! My son, who had always been a happy, shy, and quiet little boy, liked by all his teachers, was now regularly combative and defiant. His hygiene was nonexistent, and he was using drugs. Drugs were not exactly shocking since he was in high school, but our biggest concern was that he was not doing it because of peer pressure but rather that he sought it out and was doing it by himself. He would skip classes and sit in the school field, smoking weed and not hiding it. This was such a detour from who he had always been. We were shocked.

We talked to school counselors and clinical counselors everyone had the same answer for us. Each one told us that he was acting like a normal teenage boy. Our biggest frustration was because we knew that 1. he wasn't telling them the truth about what he was thinking and what was going on, and 2. because I knew my son, and this was so very far out of his character. How could we expect someone to see what was going on when they only spent an hour or so with him and don't see the struggle going on? When my son was younger, he was always so sweet and smiling. He had always been very quiet and had learning difficulties that led him to withdraw even more when in a crowd. He was always the boy on the outskirts of a game waiting to be invited.

We later found out that, in fact, what he was going through was called the prodromal stage of Schizophrenia. Prior to getting really ill, but definitely a sign of what was to come. During this time, he withdrew, experimented with drugs, and developed false beliefs. The most damaging one was that he thought everyone could hear his thoughts. He blamed me for not letting him know when he was younger so that he could learn to deal with it. It caused him so much stress and anxiety and made it very difficult for him to be around people. While arguing, at times, I would ask him what he was thinking, and he would say, "You know." I would tell him that I had no idea, but he would just get angry, and things would escalate. I knew I was losing him but didn't know what to do.

I’m not sure what it is about mothers knowing things. I guess they call it intuition, but for some reason, I always worried about this child, that something was going to go wrong. Since an episode when he was five when he told me he could hear people talking that weren't there, I had a strange sense and periodically asked him if he still heard voices.

The day came when he was living and working in a different town, an hour's drive from our home, that we found him in our basement in his old room, his eyes looking haunted, and our nightmare began. What he was saying didn’t make sense.

Within a few days, he finally started talking about what was going on and how he did indeed hear voices. He heard voices telling him how awful he was, how no one wanted him around, and how he would go to hell. How he is the worst person in the world, and everyone hates him. They were voices of people as though they were sitting close by and talking to each other about him and how they wished he wasn't there. He came home because no one wanted him. He just couldn't take it any longer. He would let me know much he hated me for not telling him that people could hear his thoughts. He felt that I didn't want him around either, but that I had to look after him because I was his mother. He believed his only option was to move to the city alone and be homeless. Our time was spent trying to reassure him and trying to figure out what we could do to help him.

When we found a program for him that helped with early psychosis intervention, we had hopes that things would soon change. He wanted help, and we hoped he would get therapy and we would find medication so he would get better. As we learned more about this disease, we also learned that those suffering often don't believe they are sick. While my son wanted help, he truly believed all of the things that his mind was telling him. He thought we were just lying again, and he was not trusting that medication would help.

We were very lucky that he was always willing to have us in his appointments with his psychiatrist and case worker. This allowed us to give our own feedback even though he often didn't believe or necessarily like what we were saying. It also let me be an advocate in times when he didn't know how to ask for another alternative to some of the medications because of how they were affecting him. Anti-psychotic meds have some terrible side effects, such as feeling tired all the time, foggy brain, drooling, excessive weight gain, and uncontrolled movement. Our attending appointments, I believe, made all the difference because we heard what was being said and could fill in important gaps.

We also participated in an education series that helped us understand more of what he was going through. On the outside, someone with Schizophrenia can seem as though they are being difficult and not doing what they need to do to get well. We learned a lot about what was happening and were able to look back and realize that his noncompliance with our household rules was, in fact, a large part of his illness.

When you get a diagnosis, first, you blame yourself. You remember every time you yelled, didn't have time, they fell and hurt themselves. You feel that you didn't do enough to make sure they felt loved and that their stress level was not overwhelming, and you find fault in everything you have ever done. You vow to do all you can to help them and get them well because you believe it was your fault.

Once you learn about the illness, you learn that no one really knows why it happens. There are some things we know, but we don't know the causes. We know that typically there are a few experiences that may have happened that could have contributed. Everyone is born with a level of vulnerability. Everyone. Then traumas, birth order/date, genetics, drug use, and environment can increase the likelihood of developing it. What you learn is that anyone can develop Schizophrenia or other serious mental illnesses, and it is not due to bad parenting. I learned that it wasn't my fault. That doesn't mean I still don't feel somewhat responsible, but it means I don't beat myself up daily because of his diagnosis. It lets us move forward.

You learn the symptoms. There are two types of symptoms, positive and negative. Positive symptoms are in addition to their daily experiences. Things like hallucinations can be tactile, auditory, and sensory. It amazes me that your mind can do such a thing as make you able to see, hear and feel things that aren't there.

These things are as real to someone with Schizophrenia as it is for you to reach out and touch them. Most have auditory hallucinations, which is what my son has. The voices are often harassing, cruel, and hateful, although, for some, they can also be very encouraging or at least start out that way.

They also develop false beliefs. These are things like believing that people are trying to poison, kill, or hurt them. A belief that others can read or hear their thoughts. A belief that everyone hates them and wants them gone. They may believe the voices are from God or the Devil, and some may believe they are Jesus or the antichrist. Some hear messages in songs, TV shows, and talk shows.

Negative symptoms are things that they lose. One thing that is very hard on loved ones is the loss of emotions and the ability to show them. Flat affect is an emotionless face that does not smile or light up anymore. It shows no joy but often shows fear in their eyes. I hear over and over about the dark, haunted eyes.

It is what I watched for daily when I saw my son. How were his eyes? Could he smile? He would also wear a hoodie with the hood up and pace a lot. These were some things I used to gauge where he was at on any given day. They can also lose some cognitive abilities and find it hard to stay focused and understand. Their mind races, and it's hard to keep it under control. They lose motivation to do things they used to love, like artwork, reading, music, and hanging out with friends. They also lose the motivation to clean up after themselves, take showers or comb their hair.

A very important thing that you learn is that recovery is possible. If your loved one works with and trusts their psychiatrist and you are lucky enough to get a good one, they can live a relatively normal life. Some can go on to earn a Ph.D. Others marry and have kids. Some work full-time jobs. Some can't, and whatever their life becomes, as long as the fear and pain are gone, that is all you can hope for. Untreated, they run the risk of irreversibly losing cognitive abilities and returning to some sense of normalcy.

Those who go on and off medication because they don't believe they really need it also run the risk of not being able to get back to their previous level of recovery. All these add stress to the caregivers, and we know they don’t see their illness as clearly as we do. To them, everything they believe is real. To us, we know it’s not.

One of the hardest symptoms to deal with is that so many don't believe they are sick. They believe everything they are seeing and hearing. And they feel all those around them are lying. They don't want to take medication but oftentimes will self-medicate with street drugs to deal with what they are experiencing.

The period that it takes to find the right medication can often take years. For some, it is quicker, but you are also fighting against the fact that perhaps they don't believe they need it or just hate the side effects so much that they will not take it properly. When you do find something that helps and they start feeling better, they want to stop because "it's all better now?" They don't believe that once off the meds, the symptoms will return, and often worse. There is no cure for Schizophrenia, only control.

When we started our journey of learning more and more about this disease, we realized hospitalization was probably in our future, but we weren't prepared for the events leading up to it. As with all parents, our hearts break when our child is hurting. We get to learn the things they do that let us know when they are struggling. We get to know the darkness in the eyes that every parent of a child with Schizophrenia knows too well. That look of being haunted. The look of hopelessness. I saw that look the day I went downstairs to find my son carving a cross into his arm. It wasn't deep, but it scared me. I insisted we go to the hospital, and he refused. I said that I would call an ambulance to come and get him if he didn't come with me, and he got into his truck and drove off.

We called the ambulance, and that is when we found out that they could not help. The only help for our psychotic child who believed everyone hated him and wanted him gone was to call the police. Days previously, I had added an app to his phone, so I could find him. We were able to give the police his exact location and when they found him, he was walking out of the Fraser River and his pants were wet up past his knees. It was January and dark.

We met him at the hospital, where the police officers took him for his own safety. When we arrived, he was in a room in a gown, and his clothing had been taken away. He was not allowed anything of his own so that he would not leave. We sat with him for hours while the police checked him in, and we waited for a psychiatrist to come and evaluate him.

As I sat with him, I wondered how it would have been for him if he was alone. How terrifying it may have been for him. Luckily the police that came were very good with him and commented about what a nice young man he was, but what if he had been terrified and fought back?

Our introduction to the psych ward was the next morning. They committed my son because he tried to hurt himself. Luckily for us, he changed his mind and didn't get swept away in the current. So now what? What was going to happen now?

As he progressed from hospital pajamas only to street clothes and then to be able to go outside for a smoke as long as he stayed on hospital property, we watched as he was "compliant" but really no better. They changed the meds he was on, and the new ones did even less for him than the first ones. The voices were loud and still vulgar and threatening. We had hoped for better.

One of the benefits of being open about your experience with mental illness is that you can learn from other people's experiences in the system. We heard from others about the lack of help in the hospital system. It is an acute focus on getting them to a place where they are no longer a risk to themselves but nothing really to help with the ongoing. There are not many places or beds available that help with therapy and consistency.

This means families often must take on the significant requirements of looking after someone with a severe mental illness. Many of us are dedicated to helping our loved ones and can focus on that. Many, however, can not leave a job to care for someone the way they may need it. Resources can be hard to find, but they are there. I will be forever thankful for the help we did receive.

Our friends and family were our support system. It's a weird thing to have to decide whether you are going to share a diagnosis, considering the stigma attached. In the psych ward, many never seemed to get visitors because either they hadn't told anyone, or the family was not supportive or believed how sick they were.

We saw our son daily. I couldn’t even bare the thought of him spending a day alone. I was determined to prove to him how much I loved him and how much he meant to me despite what the voices were telling him. We got very good at playing skip-bo and cribbage.

Once back home, we struggled with the realities of mental illness. I spent a year working from home because he would leave suddenly, not letting us know where he was going. I would get a call from my husband saying he was gone, and I would jump in the car and go find him. After trying to hurt himself, we couldn't rest if we didn't know where he was. Luckily, I worked in a place that gave me grace to work from home, and I ended up working long hours to make sure my job was completed because, at random times, he would need me to come and sit with him.

We watched a lot of TV because it helped distract him from the voices. I knew when things were tough for him because he would pace around, reading a book. He was unable to sit and focus. His attire was always jeans and a hoodie. Didn't matter the weather because the hood would go up when he felt the need to hide. He never stopped going out completely because, in his mind, he felt this was how his life was. Although he didn't like it, to him, it was his normal everyday life, so he needed to get used to it and would force himself to go.

He usually took long walks, and again during this time, I was very grateful that he was not super technical and didn't realize I could find him through his phone. We kept a very watchful eye on him after the suicide risk, and we lived terrified that we would lose him. He often used over-the-counter medications like Gravol and DM cough medicine to numb himself. They also apparently caused some hallucinations, but he was okay with them because he felt like he had control over them. He used cocaine, meth, and heroin, none of which he liked too much, thankfully, but finding needles in his drawers makes your heart sink, wondering if this was yet another illness he would have to fight and overcome.

He also had a feeling that he should be working. While I tried to encourage him to stay home and rest and let himself heal, he felt pressure to be somewhat independent, and of course, our society does look judgementally on someone who does not have a job. If he were on medication when he started a job, he would end up going off it so that he could do his job better due to the fatigue it caused. This led to a relapse losing his job, and we would start over again.

During the time while we were going back and forth with my son and his compliance with medication, his appearance and hygiene suffered. His hair was long and unwashed, his clothes were tattered and worn, and he looked a lot more like a homeless person than the smart and caring person he was.

We would go into a store together, and I would head off in the direction to get what I needed and then go and find him. I would stand back and look at people's reactions. The security guards watching him closely, and I hurt for him. I would walk up, smile, joke, and feel people's tension release. I learned a lot about myself during those times. How judgemental I could be, and we should all be more compassionate and empathetic.

He never really trusted psychiatrists, although we had one that at least he quite liked. He felt that street drugs helped him more because he thought they made him feel good instead of feeling so tired and foggy all the time. The reality was he always took a full day to recover and get back to himself after using them. They tended to increase his depression, and I could see a significant toll that they were taking on him.

He experimented with many different drugs, and each time I found some, I knew he was slowly killing himself. With the symptom of flat affect on his face, it had been over a year since I saw my son smile. That I had seen any expression on his face at all, I could see the haunting that he was going through in his eyes and the way his soul was slowly fading. I knew it was only a matter of time before he would be gone.

Between his healthcare team, his father, and myself, we knew that he had reached another crisis and he needed intervention. He was not willing to be hospitalized because he didn't trust that it would help. We had a meeting coming up with his psychiatrist, and we, as his healthcare team, had already discussed the need for him to go back to the hospital because of our fear for his safety.

I drove him to the meeting, and as we waited in the car for his father to arrive, I noticed that an RCMP officer enter the building. I immediately started to realize that my son was not going to be allowed to leave without going to the hospital, and this meeting could get really ugly. My heart sank, and I tried to fortify myself to deal with what may be coming, knowing he would be so angry, and it would break all of our hearts.

During our meeting, he brought up and discussed his desire to try Electroconvulsive therapy (ECT), which he had been researching and thought might help. His psychiatrist said it would be worth a try and something they could do in the local hospital. She also discussed his current state, and although he disagreed with her assessment at the time, he misunderstood her request for him to go to the hospital as he assumed it was for the ECT.

We went straight to the hospital, and as we sat in the emergency waiting for the hospital psychiatrist to come and meet with him, we were worried that he was confused. But at the same time did not clarify with him because I was sure he would not stay when he realized the ECT could not start right away. When the psychiatrist confirmed the ECT would take a couple of weeks to start and he wanted to leave, the psychiatrist let him know that he could not go and that if he tried, he would be stopped and committed again.

Back in the hospital, we realized that this was not going to get better unless we forced the situation. We knew that if we took him home at this point and accepted responsibility for him, nothing would likely be done, and it was suggested we refuse to take him so that the mental health care system would be required to deal with him and do more to help him get better.

We had come to a point, unfortunately, where we had to make some tough decisions. This time we knew the game, and we knew that the hospital would start trying to get us to take responsibility back. It broke our hearts to say that we wouldn't take him out for dinner or off the hospital property. We wouldn't take him home for the weekend, and he couldn't come back home and live with us. We kept insisting that he would be a risk to himself, and we were not willing to have that happen. Although we desperately wanted him home, we knew that the cycle would just continue until we forced the issue for him to get proper treatment.

So started a series of treatment facilities where he was assessed, and therapies tried. The one medication that I had seen work on him was tried again. They found a balance that seemed to work for him and that made him not too terribly tired and dealt with his depression. He started feeling a bit better but still was very fragile, and we knew if we took him home at any point that he would likely go right back off his meds.

One facility was over an hour away from our home, so we could only visit weekly. Leaving him standing at the door, knowing he just wanted to come home, was the hardest thing for us to do, but we knew we had to help him by holding fast to our belief that if we didn't do something drastic, he would no longer be around.

Once in the system and he felt better, and we started taking him off the property for dinner, we could see the beginnings of improvements. He was still extremely uncomfortable being around other people but was not hiding under his hood as much when out in public. Although we knew this was the best we could do, it still felt like abandonment on our long drive home. Many tears were shed.

The next facility was a bit closer, and I was able to spend one day during the week where we would go out and spend some time, and then on weekends, my husband and I went. Some of the facilities were locked due to flight risk and leaving was so hard. We were lucky that we lived somewhat close and could see him as much as we did. He was doing so much better that we started having him home for weekends, and although there were still some slip-ups, he knew that we supported him. He also knew that I would let the facilities know about his slip-ups.

We still said we would not take him home to live with us, and as he got better, he knew that what we had done saved him. Eventually, he came to a group home space where he has a shared apartment and 24/7 care on-site. His progress was incredible. I now got to see him smile, and he was able to have his vehicle and come home to visit daily. Eventually, he started working for a neighbor on his farm and was able to gain some confidence once again in his ability to work and do a good job.

Today he is working full-time, and while he is still in the group home, he is feeling confident that he would do well with a more autonomous living arrangement. He is the best uncle his niece and nephew could have, and they love him as much as he loves them.

The voices? They are quiet now because he is still taking his meds, but I have no doubt that if he stopped, they would be back in full force, and we would start the ride all over again. But he works with his healthcare team, and he has been able to reduce his medications enough that he is not feeling as tired. He is not dealing with his delusions to the same degree.

I have my son back. I still drive by his home when in the area to make sure his vehicle is there, and I still have him on my phone, so I know where he is, but he knows about that now, and he has me on his, so he knows where I am. I still look into his eyes every time he walks into my house, and if his hood is up, I ask if he is okay. He still will only cut his own hair, and he still wears thrift store clothing, but he smiles and laughs and works and occasionally may pick up a guitar.

I share this story with you for a few reasons.

- Trust your gut parental instincts. If you know something is wrong, don't accept answers from someone who has only spoken to your child for an hour.
- Mental illness is still a mystery to the medical world. There is so much that we don't know. So much to learn, and before we can truly help and irradicate mental illness, we must understand how it is caused—advocate for better training in medical school and more research.
- Mental illness is often thought of as just dealing with the mind and having to get that straightened out. The fact is that mental illness is a physical illness. The brain is not working properly, and it is causing issues with how your brain interprets things.
- Don't compare your journey with someone else. Everyone's journey is different, and each body needs something unique.
- Finding what works for you takes a LONGGGG time to find the right treatments. NEVER give up.
- There is always hope. Recovery can be expected, but you must understand that recovery looks different for everyone.

You are not a bad parent, sister, brother, or grandparent. You didn't cause it. There is a cocktail of environmental, traumatic situations, substances, and pre-disposed issues that can lead to a psychotic break. It can happen to anyone.

GUELDA REDMAN

Where to go for help:

British Columbia Schizophrenia Society – www.bcss.org

Early Psychosis Intervention – www.earlypsychosis.ca/

...

"Learn this from me. Holding anger is a poison. It eats you from inside. We think that hating is a weapon that attacks the person who harmed us. But hatred is a curved blade. And the harm we do, we do to ourselves."

Mitch Albom

5

FORGIVENESS

THIS IS A BIG WORD I DON'T UNDERSTAND

"In everybody's life, there's a point of no return. And in very few cases, a point where you can't go forward anymore. And when we reach that point, all we can do is quietly accept the fact. That's how we survive." Haruki Murakami

WOW! I can really breathe now. Fresh and revitalizing air. Vancouver, British Columbia, is beautiful, just like a postcard.

On a beautiful sunny August 13th, 1989, morning, stepping out of Vancouver International Airport, I am a young 22-year-old energetic Chinese girl from Hong Kong, with one hand holding a tennis racquet and one hand holding a dual cassette stereo. I am so ready to experience and achieve what I have wanted to do: Get a University Degree and become a Social Worker.

OUCH! Did a rock just fall from the sky and hit my head?

Being a good Catholic, I decided to attend mass on a Sunday morning and then meet up with my God mother's aunt for the very first time.

I have been in Canada for three weeks and decided to walk there. Yes, I can walk there. Canada Way is a nice and busy road, but maybe it was too quiet that morning!

Someone hit the back of my head with a big object. "YOU BE QUIET AND DO WHAT I TELL YOU TO DO, OR YOU WILL DIE!"

The next 30 minutes changed my life completely.

I couldn't scream, and even if I did, nobody was around to hear it. And if there were anybody around, they would think it was a domestic fight between two lovers. What!!! Not with blood pouring down from my head onto my face.

Being pushed into a van (I described later to the police it was like the van that Mr. T drove from the TV show the A-Team), the first thing I told myself was to stay awake. He (the convict) drove for about 5 minutes and then parked the van.

Still in shock and bleeding, I knew I was being captured. I was trying to get him off me, but I couldn't. I was sexually assaulted. He covered my face with a pillow, and I knew I was going to die.

Yes, I know Karate! My father insisted I learn Karate for self-defence. I fought back with all I had, kicking and punching. Nope, it didn't work and infuriated him more. I couldn't see because my face was covered with blood, but I could feel a huge object hitting my face again, again, and again. "I AM GOING TO KILL YOU BITCH!"

Don't go to sleep. Stay awake! That's what my voice inside was telling me. At one point, I could almost feel at peace when I didn't feel any pain. Am I in heaven already? Where's God? Oh yes, holding tight to the cross that my mother bought me before I left home, I felt God.

But wait, I am still alive! I know how to block. Using my left arm, I was blocking and then.... not sure how I did it, I opened the sliding door and got out of the van.

Nice Catholic Family going to church

Bright light...and honking.... What's this half-naked girl doing on the road? I felt a car pass right by me. No, it didn't stop. Then a van stopped, and a lady came out and literally picked me up and threw me into their van. She slammed the door shut, and the next thing I remembered, I was in an ambulance.

Wee oww Wee oww...sounded just like a toy ambulance I played with when I was a kid. I was still conscious. Why are they bringing me in and bringing me out and into the ambulance again? My injuries were too serious for Burnaby General Hospital to admit me. How can a hospital reject a patient? Vancouver General Hospital, here we come.

Back to this nice lady and her family. Wow, how could she do that? They happened to be on their way to church in Surrey, not Burnaby, where they found me. And the husband decided to take a different way to church that day. He stopped and reversed, then turned the other way. That is exactly where I came out! Did God send him? And he was a brand-new Catholic. They didn't care about my blood stain, and I scared the heck out of their three beautiful young children. To this day, we can't explain how it happened. But it did happen, and it was magical and spiritual. They saved me. They saved my life.

Private room in Vancouver General Hospital

I was admitted to Vancouver General Hospital in a private room for 21 days. Ten specialists and numerous nurses and lab people were there to treat me.

NO ENTRY WITHOUT CHECKING WITH THE NURSE. It's a criminal case was posted on my door.

Within two hours, he was caught. Thank God!

My injuries include head trauma, right jaw reconstruction, right eye damage, four front teeth being broken, cut lips, abdominal surgery, and bruises. I couldn't eat most of the time and could barely get up to pee. I lost over 25 pounds.

The whole time during the stay, I did not shed a tear. I felt so lucky to be alive and was too weak to even feel sad or angry. The social worker told me I could cry or be mad. I didn't have any of those emotions. There was something else in my mind that was troubling me….

Culture and Determination

Growing up, I was always pushed to the max and expected to strive and succeed. I am very thankful to my parents, who provided all they could to get me where I was. Failure or Giving Up did not exist in me.

My social worker asked if I would let my family know about my attack. I said, “No.” My sister came up from the United States to visit me, and I asked her to downplay the severity of the attack. I made her swear not to tell our parents the "whole truth."

What's the point? If they had known, they would have dragged me back home, and I would have had no chance to fulfill my dream. Still, until today, all they know is that I got robbed and beaten up, but I fought back hard and survived. I can't cry over spilled milk, so there I was, sucking it up and moving on. I refused them to visit me because of my obvious facial injuries. I had to let those scars heal up first.

College, University, Church, Marriage

I rejoined my classes shortly after my discharge from VGH. In January 1990, I started my first year at Langara College. I was so excited and took the entire course load. I was so busy handling the courses and attending weekly dental clinics for all my dental work I had no time to “grieve." That's the word my social worker kept reminding me of.

On the one day off each week, I needed to get my dental work done. I got accepted into SFU the same year and started my university journey.

Remember the nice Catholic family who saved me from my attacker? I started going to their church. There I met my husband, and he also attended Simon Fraser University. We got married in 1992. In 1996 our first son was born, and then our second son in 1999.

Focus, Focus, Focus

Despite all the visible injuries on my face, I did not stop attending classes. I didn't use any makeup, but I did grow my bangs to cover the scars. I started wearing glasses I ordered to hide my "sunk in" right eye with a scar around the corner of the eye. I had to wear temporary dentures before the bridge was put in. Occasionally I would forget to wear them and wouldn't open my mouth at school.

One of the worst things to do was to have my pictures taken. I was very photogenic before (well, that's what I was told), but even for the simple school ID, I looked terrible. I didn't know why I was still attractive enough to have anyone who would be interested in me. I was very focused on my studies, my marriage, and raising my children.

To this day, I have not talked about what happened with my family and my friends whom I met before the incident. I moved on and never mentioned a word about it. It's like the elephant in the room... my friends knew what happened, but nobody asked.

Courage, Fear, Forgiveness, Healing

I have the courage to face the physical and mental challenges, continue with my goals, have a family like normal people, and keep believing in God. I fear facing my family and some friends and embracing intimacy.

Forgiveness: This is a big word. Is it because it's been 33 years since the incident that I feel less pain? Or I have forgiven that convict? I really don't know. Or do I just try not to think about it?

Healing: It took me over 20 years to start seeing a trusted psychologist. Part of me feels like it's time to heal from my deep wounds and my fears. Another part of me feels like it's been so many years, and I have been doing fine. Why revisit? I still have conflicting views on therapy.

What do I want my readers to take from my story?

I am not a typical victim who follows the "normal" trend to a healing journey.

I have the courage to function and be okay despite the physical and emotional pain

Heal when you are ready or not ready.

Forgive when you are ready or not ready... or just forget about it.

I am a survivor, and I am living a good life. Would my life have turned out to be different if the attack didn't happen? I really don't know.

I was at the wrong place at the wrong time. I know it has strengthened my faith in God, my appreciation for the privilege of a second chance to live, and my achieving my goals. Life is good, and I intend to enjoy every moment of it.

Whatever happens in life, we must go on.

ANNA AU

...

"I let it go. It's like swimming against the current. It exhausts you. After a while, whoever you are, you just have to let go, and the river brings you home."

Joanne Harris

6

WALKING THROUGH IT
TO GET PAST IT

"Forgiveness isn't something you do for someone else. It's something you do for yourself. It's saying your not important enough to have a stranglehold on me. It saying you don't get to trap me in the past. I am worthy of a future." Jodi Picoult

My mother and father came from abusive families. My father being indigenous, his father (my grandfather) went to a residential school and drank heavily to cope with the memories of his time there. He had multiple families and fathered 16 children. My father has memories of him being a great musician who loved to play guitar and sing when he was sober. My father grew up very poor and sold drugs at a young age, and then he turned to stealing.

He married young, trying to make the family he had always desired, but it quickly fell apart. He moved to Victoria, British Columbia, to start fresh, and this is where he met my mother.

My mother was born to a mother who didn't want kids and was named after her father's mistress. Her father moved out and became a truck driver, and her mother had two more girls with a new man. My mother became responsible for the younger two while her mother drank and had sex with men while the girls were locked in a closet.

Her mother tried to drown her, and at the age of 11, my mother broke a window and cut her wrists open in front of her mom in hopes of being taken away from the responsibility of caring for her siblings and the abuse.

It worked, and she was taken to a group home for troubled teens. She was in and out of homes, and then at 17, she ran away with one of her sisters and found herself pregnant a year later. She had to drop out of school. Her sister was prostituting, and my mother would steal from her to pay the bills.

She married her child's father in hopes of escaping the street life and building a family of her own. When my oldest sister was born, her father decided he didn't want her and left my mother. Nineteen a dropout and responsible for a child.

My mother didn't know what to do and turned to her grandparents for help. They took custody of my sister for a year while my mother got back on her feet. My mother moved to Victoria, BC, and met my father. My father and she worked at the same job cleaning up biohazards (human remains). Both lived in the same apartment building. They quickly fell in love, and my mother decided it was time to bring my sister to Victoria so they could all be a family together.

In the next two years, they had my two brothers, sixteen months apart. My oldest brother was very premature and almost didn't survive. He's had the hardest go at life right from the beginning and still to this day.

My mother and father's relationship at this point became strained due to my father abusing my siblings. Two years later, my mother became pregnant again. When she did get pregnant, it was me in her tummy this time, and the doctors had told my mother there was a chance I was going to be born with multiple health conditions Hydrocephalus and Spina Bifida were mentioned, and my mother was offered a late-term abortion for quality-of-life purposes. Mother decided to keep the pregnancy going, but my father did not want me after hearing I would most likely be disabled. One evening during an argument, he said, "I don't want a retarded child or one in a wheelchair," and in disgust, my mother spit in his face.

Father retaliated by throwing a five-pound ashtray at my mother's stomach. My mother called the police for help that night, and she was then arrested for antagonizing the fight by spitting. She spent time in jail and was released on my due date of June 22.

My mother gave birth to me the next day. Alone and when the doctor ordered an emergency cesarian due to my heart rate dropping, she was awake through it and so brave. My umbilical cord was twice wrapped around my neck, and I was blue. The doctor cut the cord off my neck, and I began to breathe and cry.

My first weeks were full of testing and hospital visits. Supervised visits with my dad to pick my name where he suggested "Charity" because f**k that baby he didn't want. My mother settled on Emily on her own. I was a healthy baby, unlike the doctor predicted, and mom brought my siblings home to be with me soon after. She started working at a restaurant to pay the bills.

We had a babysitter for a while, but my father would stalk this young girl on her way home, so she soon quit leaving my mother with no one to help her. She needed my father's help, and soon she let him back in the house.

During my toddler years, my mother noticed some things that were different about me, the way I didn't talk at all at two or respond to my name, I didn't make eye contact, I walked on my toes, I would sway my head and flap my arms. I wouldn't wear clothes because of the way they felt against my skin, I hated food textures, and breast fed until I was four years old. My mother took me to the pediatrician, and I was diagnosed at the time with Asperger's syndrome, which we now call Autism Spectrum Disorder or ASD.

We moved to Manitoba that same year and my parents had my younger sister. It seemed like suddenly my diagnosis was forgotten and so was I. I never got any sort of support to help me cope in a world not meant for someone with sensory issues and cognitive delay, among other things. I found it extremely difficult to learn to care for myself, and suffered hygienically as well as nutritionally for years.

At three or four, I remember my family living in a small house on a farm with acreage. We had animals, and as children, we took part in the care and upkeep of them. I enjoyed this so much and would wake up super early every day just to feed the chickens before my mom would leave for work.

Both my parents had struggles with their own family lives growing up and struggled at times to know how to raise and cope with five children while still growing themselves which left us neglected and abused. With the stress of their marriage as well as financial issues we found ourselves moving off the farm and into a house in a bad part of town. I remember my first Christmas in this house, someone was murdered just two doors down. My parents soon after left Manitoba to start better lives for us.

When we moved to British Columbia, I was almost six. We lived in the motel sharing one bed for all of us kids for months until my parents found a house. It was small white and crooked. we had rabbits as pets and raised several animals such as an old dog named Gertie, and an injured hawk. This is the house I lived in when I started Kindergarten.

I was under weight, didn't talk, and would have accidents. So, I was very prone to be bullied which made the accidents worse and I completely stopped eating for days at a time. As a young child I developed disordered eating patterns, my stomach hurt all the time due to an undiagnosed stomach disease and my teeth had soft enamel when they grew in due to malnutrition.

My parents divorced when I was seven due to my father's abuse and my mother started dating someone who had severe mental health issues and a crack addiction. He would come into my room at night and try to sleep in my bed. He would touch me between the legs, as I pretended to sleep, and then he would leave.

The physical abuse from him toward my mother got so bad. I witnessed my mother being physically and sexually assaulted by this man on multiple occasions. He threw her down the front stairs of our house and she broke her foot ending her up in the hospital for several months getting a bone replaced, and plates put in her heel. We stayed at her friend's house who was luckily an all right guy with a normal job and wife and two kids.

When we went back with my mom it was to move into the basement of a house on the reserve, my four siblings and I sharing one room and my mom sleeping on a foam pad on the floor. It was so rough growing up, but on the reserve, we always had kids to play with, a forest to make forts, and dogs to chase. My mother started selling weed and worked as a roofer during the day when we were in school. Eventually, we got a nicer place. A townhouse with a yard and a room for my mom. This was the best year of my life.

She then met whom I call my stepfather for the sake of the story, but he never married my mother, and I'm glad as hell he didn't. They were together for six years, and parts of this story are during their relationship. He was almost 300 pounds, 6 feet tall, and a drunk. They separated on July 1st, 2012.

My best friend had asked me the night before if I'd like to go to Vancouver for the day and see a concert that evening with her and her aunties. I'd never gone to a concert or to the city without my parents. So, I was super excited when my mom said I could go.

We left super early that morning, stopping along the way to pick up lunch to eat on the beach.

I collected sea glass and shells; we smoked and enjoyed our lunch. I ate an edible for the second time ever. We spent the day exploring downtown, window shopping, and eating snacks.

That evening at the concert, I found out we were not sitting with her aunties at all but 20 rows up. There were two men in the seats next to ours. As the concert got on, we sang the songs, we danced, and generally were having an amazing time. We stole someone's hard lemonade.

I hesitated at first, being cautious in public but gave in because I wanted to be fun. I started feeling sick. I don't know if it was the edibles, the hard lemonade or if I had been drugged by the drinks. Or everything together, but I felt like I was going to die.

My friend and I went to the bathroom quickly as the concert ended. I threw up hard and banged my head into the side of the stall. Unable to keep my balance for a second. We staggered to the vehicle unnoticed by the aunties as they were drinking too and the person who was driving was preoccupied with getting everyone to the vehicle safely and out of the crowd now trying to leave the stadium.

I laid my head on the window. I could feel the cold glass on my cheek as we rattled along the highway in the darkness. We pulled into town, and I asked to be dropped off at my house. I didn't have keys, and I didn't know if anyone was home, but I just wanted to lay in my bed and go to sleep.

I walked up to our townhouse door, and to my surprise, I was greeted by my older brother and his friend hanging out in the yard. Both were high on something and were pacing about talking to each other. The door was locked, and all the lights were off inside. Either my mother wasn't home, or everyone had gone to bed early, which was weird for a summer night. My first thought was to go to a neighbor's house and ask to use their landline to call my mom to come open the door. The phone rang, but no one answered. I walked back to the front door and waited.

At this point, it was starting to get light outside, and I could feel the drinks in my stomach, heavy like rocks. On my hands and knees, I threw up everything I'd ever eaten, the acid coming out my nose, the cement cutting into my knees. My brother left, not wanting to be the one to greet my mother when she got home to the sight of me sick on the doorstep.

After what seemed like ages, my mother's vehicle finally pulled into the parking lot, music blaring out the windows, and her and my stepfather screaming at each other like usual. He was abusive in the past, breaking my mother's eye socket. Because of that situation, there was a no-contact order was established, and regardless, he was still living in the home with us. She forgave him. My mother always tried to normalize the abuse in all her relationships with men by saying she deserved it or that they had their reasons to hurt her.

And on that night, they stumbled to the door, surprised to see fourteen-year-old me doubled over on the ground surrounded by vomit. Without hesitation or questioning, my mother picked me up and carried me up the stairs to my room and tucked me into bed like a baby. This would be the very last time my mother tucked me into bed and the last night of my childhood.

My mother continued partying and drinking with my stepfather in the kitchen while I and my little sister slept upstairs.

Suddenly I am awake, the morning sun coming in my window and hitting my face. The music was shut off now. Screams seemed to radiate through the floor. I could hear my mother's voice louder than the others screaming "GET THE F**K OUT" over and over, then a series of loud bangs, and it got quiet.

Knowing how aggressive my stepfather had been in the past with my siblings and my mother, I was afraid for my mother's life! I got to my feet and ran. At the top of the landing, looking down I could see my mother laying halfway up the stairs pinned by her throat, not struggling, her eyes black and glassy. My stepdad, on top of her choking her already limp body.

With every last ounce of energy I had in me while sick and drunk, I jumped on top of him, swinging, my fists colliding with the side of his head. I scratched at his face, trying to gouge out his eyes. Maybe if he couldn't see, he wouldn't be able to defend himself.

Panicking to save my mother and my hands covered with blood, I wrapped my hands around his neck and strangled him hard. Releasing years of pent-up anger toward him for the abuse.

Letting go of her throat, he grabbed my hands from his neck, spinning around to attack me.

Quickly I head-butted him in the face, blood spraying from his nose; he hesitated. I turned around and ran through the living room to the back, trying to open the sliding glass door toward the yard, followed by him. I hopped over the fence and ran across the street to the playground.

He screamed my name over the fence, "EMILY YOU BITCH!" And then he was gone. Obviously scared of the repercussions of his actions.

Sitting on the swing, I started hearing my name being yelled. At first, it was my little sister's voice and then my mother's. They were outside looking for me or my body at this point in fear that the fight had continued outside, and I had been left beaten somewhere.

I sat on the swing for a minute longer, still in my pajamas, still covered in blood. I could hear the sirens coming, and a sense of peace filled my heart. Maybe this would be the time he would be arrested and not come back to hurt us more, my mother would finally be free because she couldn't give in if he was locked up. Then my chest tightened. Panic set in as I remembered what the house had been hiding this whole time. The grow op.

The house was suddenly swarming with police cars. I got up from the swing, walked back to the fence, and climbed over. Walking back into the house, I saw my mother sitting on the chairs near the front door where I had been laying only a few hours earlier. Blood ran down her face, and bruises started to show around her neck. She sobbed loudly, her hands cuffed together but holding a tea towel to her head to stop the bleeding.

I walked up to my room, climb into bed, and pulled the covers up over my face. A knock at the door startled me, and before I could say anything or get up to open it myself, a female police officer and a social worker were entering my room. “You need to get some clothes together and a bag. Do you have a bag? We need you to come with us.” I stood there quietly. My feet felt like they were melted into the carpet as I tried to gather an outfit and some clean socks before shoving them into my school bag.

“Can I change alone?” I asked the woman standing in my room. “We can step out, but you’ll have to leave the door cracked, so we can make sure you don’t grab any weapons” I was protecting my mom. Am I being arrested? Are they taking us away? They left the room. I put on a dirty t-shirt of my mother’s and a pair of black jeans. Walking out of my room I could see the grow op door open the plants tall and near harvest. The smell filled the hallway.

In the parking lot of the townhouse, six police cars waited, and I was ushered into the back of one, and my younger sister was already inside holding a bag herself. So, they were taking us away. We were driven to the police station and brought into an interview room. We were told to wait there until they could find somewhere for us to go.

The hours went by slowly, and we both fell asleep on the floor. No blankets, no pillow. The next morning, I woke up still in the police station. Locked into the interview room. I banged on the door, but nobody came. That afternoon woman appeared. A police officer unlocked the door with a smirk on his face.

We were first transferred to the aboriginal foster care office and then taken to a motel. We stay there for a few days. It was the same hotel my older sister worked at. She didn't do room service calls usually, but when I found out there was a computer in the motel lobby, I went to message her on Facebook to tell her to come to see us that night when we ordered dinner.

That night she came into the room with our food, and we played it like we didn't know each other. She smiled and left. I asked to run to the kitchen for something else and met my sister in the hallway. We embraced, and for a second, I felt safe. We continued this routine during the time we spent at the motel so at least our sister could relay to our mom that we were safe and together.

Eventually, we were given to my older sister so she could care for us while my mom got back on her feet. Since the house was raided, trashed, and ransacked by neighbors, and then we were evicted the day my mom got out of holding at the jail.

I started drinking more and would run off with my friend for several nights at a time. I went camping with some friends at the river one night and was assaulted in a camper and then had my clothing and shoes burned. I walked back to my sister's apartment in my friend's shirt, barefoot and bruised.

That same night my mother came to visit us. Her eyes were wide like the full moon. She talked fast and was sweating, telling us about her next scheme to get us back when her phone rang. She asked me to go for a walk with her, and I did. A man in a jeep pulled up next to us while we were walking and handed my mom something. She got into his vehicle, and they drove off. I walked back alone and waited for her on the step of the apartment where I was staying with my sister.

The jeep pulled back up, and she got out. "That's my new boyfriend," she exclaimed. Holding out her hand, revealing a small baggy with a tiny white rock inside.

Spring 2014

My eyes jumped open, hearing my phone ring so early in the morning, scrambling to find it in a mess of sheets. Answering it and hearing the words, "Your mom is dead; I'm coming to get you right now." The room spun, and my hands went ice cold. The light faded from my eyes like the lights at beginning of a play. The show was about to begin.

I picked up my clothes from the night before, tossed them on, running to the door, begging to be let outside. Not sure if I was even awake or not. This had to be a dream. A red car came into the parking lot, blaring the horn. The drive seemed like it took five seconds, and we came screeching to a stop in front of my mother's building. I ran straight into what I can only describe as one of my worst nightmares.

My mother's lifeless body lay on the lobby floor. Blood poured from her mouth and nose, her skin a pale blue. Her favorite shirt was stained with blood and vomit, cut up the middle to expose her chest. Emergency personnel surrounded her body as it convulsed with every shock of the paddles. Empty needles that once contained life-saving medicine, dirty gauze, and medical equipment seemed to make a mosaic background to the macabre scene.

The neighbors, at this point, had either seen what was happening on their way out to work or had heard the sirens outside and gathered on the stairs well, and a crowd began to form outside the glass door.

With a slight pulse and shallow breaths, her body was carried out on a stretcher. A scream of agony as loud as the sirens left my mouth, and I toppled to the ground. Suddenly unable to feel my legs, the neighbor grabbed my arm, lifted me to my feet, hugged me, and I climbed into the ambulance. I road with her, I held her hand and whispered to her to keep fighting. Just please hold on for me and my siblings. I can't do this on my own, I said, squeezing her hand. I laid my head down on her chest and prayed to whatever power there is to not take her. The doors burst open, and a dozen nurses ran to our side. She was wheeled into a large room and hooked up to a dozen machines.

The doctor came in to speak with me. "Your mom may have suffered brain damage from loss of oxygen, we don't know whether she's going to wake up just yet, but I do suggest you gather your family together to say their goodbyes just in case. "I'm so sorry." My heart fell to pieces looking at my mother in the hospital bed. I tried to think of what I was going to say to my family, them going about their mornings, blissfully unaware.

I called my father first, the words squeezing my throat almost closed as they came out

"Mom overdosed, and she died this morning. She's on life support now. I need you to bring the rest of the kids to say goodbye I don't know what's going to happen, but they said she might not make it." The line was silent. Suddenly I could hear my dad screaming in the other room for my grandmother, and then the phone cut off. My father drove as fast as he could and, for once, seemed like he cared about my mother. They were divorced for years at this point.

My brother was unable to even go into the room where my mother was. Afraid to see her in the state she was in. My younger sister, the baby of the family, went in alone, with no one wanting anyone to see her cry. And then my father asked to go in, which I never expected him to do. I may never know what he said in those moments alone, but I hope they were loving and kind.

After a few hours of us waiting together, my siblings and father went home for the night. I went to a friend's to eat and gather myself. I'd been crying all day and just needed a second to breathe.

I had only been gone an hour or so when the hospital called my cell phone. "She's awake! And she's asking where you are." I was shocked. Minutes ago, I was mourning my mother, who was suffering from brain damage, and now I was being told she was awake and talking. I got on my friend's bike and went back to the hospital.

My mother was pacing about when I walked into the hospital room, muttering about wearing a diaper and how her favorite shirt had been ruined and cut up. I was furious that she didn't seem to care that she almost died. I was almost about to start yelling when the nurse came in to speak with us together. And a social worker in tow.

"I understand you've been living on your own for some time. Emily and your partner and you have a place together? Is there any chance your mother could go home with you? Otherwise, she'll have to stay here until we feel she's safe alone at home?" The words felt like a slap to the face.

It was only a few months short of my 18th birthday, and I had been living apart from my mother because she was using, and social services wouldn't take me and my sister away from her. I left to keep myself safe, and now they wanted me to care for her. I sadly agreed to take her home.

She was wearing green hospital pajamas and a scarf the hospital had given her, there was snow on the ground, and it was dark outside. We walked along the roadside, unable to walk on the frozen sidewalk most of the way. She stopped every few blocks to get sick and complain about not wanting to stay with me. I didn't want her to stay with me either, so I guess it was even.

The place I was staying was not suitable for someone who just overdosed to be. I was staying at a boyfriend's brother's house while he was in jail for graphic things, I cannot mention due to their nature. But I can say there were drugs in the house, and it just wasn't a place for my mother to stay. It lasted not even a full night when I awoke to my mother trying to break into where the drugs were kept.

"YOU WERE DEAD THIS MORNING!" I shouted at her in the darkness of the back room. I grabbed her arm and drug her to the front door, pushing her out into the snow and throwing her scarf and shoes off the balcony. I was so broken. How could she even think of using again after what had happened? How could she put us through that again? Mother and I stopped talking after this for many months, she has tried to come back into my life, and I wish I could let her, I wish she could be a grandmother to my children, but we deal with the cards we are dealt.

2015

My mom went to jail and left me to care for my younger sister for several days before the ministry realized we were home alone. I luckily was given a foster mom, like a guardian angel, who would come stay with us and help me do the grocery shopping and budget. I turned to selling drugs and working part-time while in school to pay for the bills.

The support from the government took a while to come, and my mental health spiraled. One day my foster parent and sister went for a walk, and I wrapped an extension cord around the ceiling fan. I climbed up on top of my dresser and was ready to jump off when my guardian angel came swooping back into the house. "I had a feeling I needed to come back for you."

This single moment of kindness stopped me. It made me realize there were people there who still cared for me. I wasn't alone left to deal with the world. I had a few select people who were on my side. My foster mom has stuck by my side and chosen to be there for me in place of my mother, who no longer could hold all her trauma together for her kids.

I regret how I reacted that night with my mother now. As an adult, I think about it often. Pushing her out in the snow, My cruel words, and my reaction. Angry and unable to think straight. My mother dealt with so much trauma my whole life, and I used to blame her for choosing drugs over us, it ruined a lot of my childhood and young adult life, and as a traumatized adult myself, I've realized she uses the drugs to numb the pain to keep on living every day and without them, she would surely have committed suicide years ago. She's not how I remember. But she's surviving for us as best as she can with the tools she was given.

Later in 2015

Right before I graduated high school, my boyfriend at the time, who was older than me and a drug dealer, got me pregnant. He would walk me to and from school, I wasn't allowed to go out, he locked me in the house when he had work, and I didn't have school, and often he would leave for the weekend, leaving me locked inside, pregnant, and sick.

I would scrounge for anything to eat, bread crust, old takeout, leftover anything. I was given breakfast and lunch at school most days, so when I was home locked inside, I would starve. The baby growing in my belly made me feel like I was dying, and I threw up constantly. It was late August, and two things were getting bigger, my belly and the arguments. I got into a fight with that partner, I don't even remember what it was about, but he threw me against the door frame of our room, pushing me by my growing belly, the back of my head and my spine hitting the frame and I crumpled to the ground. He gave me a hard swift kick to the stomach, and the fight was over.

I lay there on my bedroom floor, half in the hallway and in pain. Something felt off. After hours of nausea and back pain, blood and crying. I was left home alone. Weak, I crawled to the bathroom, and I sat on the toilet, bleeding down my legs, and as I looked down, I saw the fetus in the toilet. He was gone. I touched his hand, terrified. I went to the hospital alone. I named the baby Thomas Andrew B. He never got to see the world, but for a few short months, we knew each other while he grew and stretched and kicked at my belly, and I love him to this day. I was released the same night and spent four days locked in my bedroom as a punishment for losing the baby.

After this, the abuse got worse, my panic attacks became crazy, and all my hair started to fall out.

I graduated high school a year late but finished and was so proud of all the stuff I made it through to get to that point.

2016

I was locked inside ninety percent of the time. We rarely had food. I didn't see my family and I wasn't allowed to go see my friends. There were cameras all over the house. I couldn't use the bathroom without someone watching. One morning, clearly just fed up and not a thing to lose, I started a fight to try and leave, but the doors had locks on both sides, and I needed a key to get out.

The commotion woke up one of the other people who recently had started staying in the house, and he luckily called the police and told them that I had been locked inside for months, and he was scared to confront the person doing it. The police showed up within minutes. They broke the door open, and I collected a backpack of belongings as fast as I could. I took two outfits, my teddy bear, and my make-up case, and that's it. I left to stay at my parent's house on the floor and never looked back. Four days after I escaped, that roommate who helped me hung himself in his room and wasn't found until days later.

While living in Hope with my family, I started working full-time. I was drinking every night, went to parties, and making friends. I was free for the first time in almost five years. I got a job working on a movie set as a background actor and managed a pizza restaurant at night. I had been using dating sites on and off, and nothing seemed to come of it. Until one night, as I was closing, the crew for the film came to buy some pizzas. I reluctantly let them in and fired back up the oven. Knowing how late everyone was working, I just wanted to feed people.

A familiar face walked into the restaurant, and I said, "I think I know you. We matched online." He became red in the face and asked for the bathroom keys. His work buddies laughing, asked me for my phone number to give him because they knew he was single, and I gave it to them because he seemed sweet. We hung out together in town until filming finished, and on his last day, we lay on the dock of the lake in the sun and talked about me going to see him as soon as he was back from his next work trip.

I started visiting him in the city, and within a month, he had given me a credit card to spend on his dime and asked me to move to the city with him, and I did. It was a month into our relationship living together when he asked me to move back out because he wasn't ready to live together. So, I started working and found a place. Two days short of me moving in, I found out I was pregnant. I jokingly took a test, not thinking it would be positive, and sure enough, two very bold lines showed on the test. He suddenly asked me to not move out and to please stay with him as a family.

During my pregnancy, I was diagnosed with Hyperemesis Gravidarum. For eight months, I couldn't keep anything down, water, crackers, electrolytes. Nothing. Everything came up as fast as it went down. My stomach burned with acid, my legs ached, my hair fell out, I had a bloody nose, and my teeth fell out. All while growing a baby in my body and not being sure the baby would make it because I had lost a baby in the past. Pretty soon, I stopped sleeping. I became bitter and afraid that this was all going to be for nothing, I just wanted to be a family, and I was scared it was going to be taken away.

My back started hurting so badly that I spent three days on the couch, not eating or moving. The next night I suddenly awoke to a gush. I flicked on the light to discover myself covered in blood. It was happening again….

We hurried to the hospital. I was hooked up to all the machines, and I could see the tiny heartbeat going on the monitor. For a second, everything stopped. This was my family. This was my big moment. The baby came into this world at 9:49 pm. Six weeks early and screaming like the little warrior I hoped she was going to be. When she was placed in my arms, all the resentment, anger, and sadness melted away and was replaced with such utter love for the baby and the family I made all on my own.

2017

When my daughter was born, she was early from stress but healthy, and since that day, her father has done everything to take her from me. We went to family counseling, and for a while, I thought we were doing better. My mood was still terrible, but I was coping. I love being a mom. I just couldn't settle into the role of middle-class housewife with an unsupportive husband who didn't understand complex trauma and Autism. I'd never done it before, and I didn't have anyone to learn it from. My parents are divorced, and my daughter's father's parents are divorced. No one sticks together these days, but I was determined to make this family work.

2019

My trauma became too much as a new mother. I became angry and wanted to leave, and my daughter's father chose to take her and leave to protect himself from me leaving first. I was unable to function in a stable environment. I couldn't be with someone who didn't understand the panic attacks, the night terrors, the anxiety.

Again, I began drinking heavily at night to cope, and because I'd never had stability in my life and constantly felt out of place, the trauma was too much, and I was falling apart. I had been in protection mode for so long. I lost my job, my house, and my health. I was in and out of the hospital for bone and blood infections.

After my daughter was taken by her father, it's taken four years for me to get back on my feet with dedication and strength, different medications, therapy, and love.

Epilogue

Feeling stable is an integral part of my good mental health and the growth I've experienced since high school. The maturity and stability I've achieved on my own proved to me that I wasn't ready at 18 to be a parent. Losing Thomas was a terrible blessing because I was able to escape and heal, make a family in a safer environment, and provide my children with stability, love, and support.

We couldn't live together, my older daughter's dad and me. We both needed to mature and learn to survive alone. I never thought I could ever survive another pregnancy either, but years later, I did do it again. For my second daughter and with my very best friend, who does his best to understand me, loves me with my condition, and loves my first daughter like his own child. I do my best to make a family home we all can grow and feel safe. While I heal from my unfortunately tragic and abusive childhood.

I love my daughters and their dads, and having them, both become my family has made life so much fuller. It's tough at times to raise kids while co-parenting. We often don't get along, but the reward of having my children have a better life than me, having all these people who love them, makes all the pain and grief worth it.

These situations changed who I was drastically growing up and had an impact on my ability to choose a safe partner and trust. It broke my family, and my siblings went their own ways. We all dealt with the trauma of losing the mom we used to have, and often find that we each have our own version of how things took place. All I can do is be true to my memories and hope that sharing my story will make a difference to someone. Knowing that I would have missed these beautiful children I made had I not been here. That my kid's fathers would not have their families makes me cry every time I think about it.

Almost losing my mom has made me realize I would never want to leave my children wondering why they weren't good enough for me to be strong and keep fighting for them. I spent so much of my life wondering why I wasn't good enough for my mom to try harder, but she did try for as long as she could, and that's all I can hope to do as well. Try for as long as I can. I may never heal from the trauma, and the night terrors may never go away, but I can control how I respond to the trauma and how I choose to make my life look outside of it. I am persistent to do better than my parents. I had to walk through the trauma to get through it and move on with my life.

I recently started acting again and volunteering, trying to find things outside of being a mom that is part of my identity because the trauma was all the identity I had, and then I became a mom, and that took over. Learning to do things for myself, take care of my needs, and put myself and my children first has helped me emphasize.

The true meaning of life for me is loving and being loved and having these kids to carry on that love when we're all long gone.

My life's been crazy, but I still hope to make my children proud.

EMILY CRONK

...

"Resilience is accepting your new reality, even if it's less good than the one you had before. You can fight it, you can do nothing but scream about what you've lost, or you can accept that and try to put together something that's good."

Elizabeth Edwards

7

A TALE OF A GIRL WHO WAS MADE TO FEEL SHE WASN'T WORTHY

YET SHE STILL FOUND HER WAY

"You and only you are ultimately responsible for who you become and how happy you are."
Rachel Hollis

I was standing on my deck, the mist was coming off the mountain behind grandma's house, and the smell of wood stove smoke hung thick in the air. It was a chilly dark evening. There I stood, shaken from the events that had just taken place. The feelings of anger and sadness rushed through me. And I was replaying the event in my head, thinking, why does this keep happening to me?

My clothes and school stuff are thrown out the door just like worthless trash, just like me. My 14-year-old brain is on fire, yet how is it that I feel everything in my stomach? It's as if a heavy stone was suddenly placed in the pit of my stomach and throat. I collect my things and make the quick walk over to grandma's house.

My savior! What would I have done without my grandma living so close to us? I think as I look down the dark logging road, and fear comes over me as I imagine having to hitchhike to town to make it to my closest friend's home, which is 15 km away along the famous Highway of Tears.

You really never know what comment or action will set Mother off. Sometimes she will just laugh stuff off. Tonight wasn't one of those nights.

It all started with my air cadet gear. Mother " pick up your clothes. You're such a slug, you know that, right?!" I don't care how I hang the clothes; instead of hanging them on the hanger, I just throw them on the hook. This carelessness causes the clothes to fall.

Mother comes back from the kitchen." what the f**k Noella! You disrespectful little bitch. I told you to f**king hang up your clothes, get the f**k out here and do it now." Me not knowing they fell down. Call back, mom. I did hang them up.

Mother was now raging, " does it look like the f**king clothes are hung up? Are you f**king stupid?" I come to pick up the clothes again. I sassily say "sorry" as I'm picking up the clothes. At that moment, with my head down, grabbing the clothes, I feel a fist connect with my face. Mother, "how dare you f**king sass me? When I ask you f**king do something, I mean to do it."

Shocked, I started crying and asked, "What was that for?" Mother, "you know what the f**k you did? You know what?! You think it's so bad here, and I'm such a terrible Mother. Why don't you get the f**k out? I gave three other children up for adoption. What makes you think that you're so special?" "Oh, don't worry. I know I'm not special," I managed to say.

Safely at grandma's, she hugs me and says, "you know you're not supposed to say things that will upset your mother. She has her dry drunk moments and is still healing from her past pains, and you know this." My parents have been together since my dad was 19. So, grandma has dealt with my mother's manic mood swings for a while now.

Grandma's house is almost sickeningly warm. I lay my head in her lap, and we fall into our routine. Having done this so many times before, we don't say anything. She just rubs my head and pops a peppermint in my mouth. My grandma finally broke her silence by saying, " we should say a prayer." So, we start with the Our Father and end with Hail Mary. My grandma throws in an extra prayer for my mother. Praying she finds peace and a way to speak kindly.

Tears are falling silently again. For my mothers, harsh words have become a mantra on repeat in my head. "You're not special, your worthless, little bitch, so f**king stupid, slug." Quickly wearing away at my confidence and self-esteem. The darkness and hatred for myself grew each day.

My father is due home in a few days. I dread what's to come. I hate how he just takes her side. Does he even understand what it feels like to be called those names?

A memory of my mother screaming the ugliest things at my father as she walked down the logging road for the highway, her duffel bag slung around her back. Does he think it's normal? He has a work ethic like no other but doesn't have the energy to deal with anything when he comes home from camp on Fridays. So, we begin the dance of my mother crying to my father about how awful we children were to her all week.

He'll also give me shit, then come to my grandmas to tell me to go back home. However, this time I'd had enough. My teenage brain was becoming more resistant. This has happened too often, and I didn't want to return.

My dad's middle brother came over for a visit and asked about childcare, and my ears perked up! Sadly, my cousin's mother left them, and he needed someone to be able to stay at the house as he would be working shift work. This kickstarted my first-ever nanny job, where I was paid $20.00 a day to take care of three children, ages six, seven, and eight.

During this time, I was humbled by how negatively my mother's parenting style impacted me. My six-year-old cousin said, "I want to heat up this pasta." I told her to use the microwave. I was using the family computer.

Suddenly I heard the microwave sparking like metal was in there. I ran to the kitchen, and my cousin was standing there in shock. She had put the whole pot in the microwave! I started to scream. "What the f**k were you thinking," just fell out of my mouth. I quickly hit the open button, the door swings open, and some smoke bellows out.

She starts to cry, " why are you yelling at me? I'm just a child; I don't know any better." That snapped me out of my angry mindset and caused me to pause. Still upset, she ran to her room.

I collected my thoughts for a moment and thought, wow, I really overreacted there. Why? Well, I guess I was scared, yes, scared. I work out in my head. Once I had that figured out, I found my cousin teary-eyed lying in her bed. "Get out!" she screams at me.

When I speak, I'm quiet and calm. "I'm so sorry I yelled at you back there, I was just so scared, and it came out like that. I know you are just learning." My cousin repeats, " I know I'm just a child. I didn't know any better." "You're right, sweetheart, you are, and I'm sorry, I didn't specifically tell you what to heat your noodles up in. So next time, let's use a glass bowl. I'm going to try really hard not to yell next time I get scared, okay?"

This was the first time I became aware of how I was unknowingly starting to do the same learned behavior I was trying to escape from in my mother.

Life was better at my uncle's, even though I didn't have a room and slept on the couch. It felt safe. During this time, I continued to have contact with my mother. Mainly through phone conversations, I'd need help cooking something for the children, and the logical thing would be to call my mother. Even though I endured years of mental and physical abuse from her, I still couldn't manage to cut her out of my life entirely. I'd ration with myself that she didn't know better. She had a hard life growing up. It's hard for her to love because she wasn't shown how.

In this particular conversation, she explained how she makes her dinner rolls. I sketched down the recipe on some scrap pieces of paper by the phone. After I got it written, I was about to say goodbye, and she mentioned my brothers got an apartment together in Thornhill close to our high school. My one brother was in grade ten, and I was in grade eight. And my oldest brother, who just moved here with us a few years ago. He has schizophrenia, and my other was having a hard time dealing with him. Even though he was medicated, he talked differently and would ramble on with these interesting stories.

However, to my mother, these stories were like nails on a chalkboard. Over time she couldn't handle it anymore and found the boys a place to stay. My teenage brother was meant to take care of him while on medication.

I was excited that they would be close to my school so I could go hang out. My brother also seemed cool and edgy to me, and I liked hangout with his friends. My mother asked how I was doing in school. I told her how I was doing well.

I have always loved school! Even at a young age. The school was my escape, a place where I was well-liked and spoken to kindly (most of the time, hurting children tends to hurt others). I wasn't immune to the impact of bullies.

My grades were amazing even though I suffer from dyslexia. Reading, writing, and math were a struggle; however, I was determined to learn, and I never gave up, no matter how hard something was. It was at this high school that I found my best friend. She happened to move here to live with her dad. He lived close to my uncle's house! Thankfully she was a rock star student like I was, as my uncle had high expectations for my friends to be able to come over to the house. They had to hold a place on the honor roll, and my friend was always at the top!

Now here's the part where my life starts to get a bit spicy. Even though I was a good student and so was my friend doesn't mean we were immune to the infection of being a young teenager in a small town. Both of us girls were hurting differently and could empathize with each other. Our mothers were similar to each other.

I struggled to feel loved and have self-worth because I was still filled with so much hurt. My mother's words of hate were never far from my ears. I needed to drown them out. Being a petite 14-year-old doesn't take much to get you drunk.

My brother's apartment became the favorite hangout place. Close to the school and corner store. There was also a pub and liquor store nearby. All it would take for my friend and I to get wasted was one 2 L bottle of a cooler. The cost was $10.00, half a day's wages for being a live-in nanny for my uncle.

When that numbness washed over me, I would finally feel nothing and everything at the same time. My senses were all over the place at one moment, happy and laughing the next, crying and retelling a sad story I had kept secret for too long.

At first, my young body could mostly handle these nights of drinking till I blacked out. I'd maybe feel uneasy the next day, yet each time I drank, my recovery would become longer and harder. It got way worse when I started to drink hard alcohol. Drinking so much, I'd be so sick and drunk the following day. No matter how poisoned I was or how many times I cried the next day, I'm never drinking again. Even though my mother is a recovering alcoholic, I knew the dangers.

I still did it anyways. Why? Because it's socially acceptable, was fairly easy to get, and it was a cheap fix to mask the hurting. I made friends with some of the older people who lived in the horseshoe-shaped apartment complex. Surprisingly I was always safe. None of these people we befriended were into heavily intoxicated teenage girls. I suffered more at my own hand, meaning I was careless with my body and my heart. So desperate to feel loved.

My first consensual sexual experience was with my boyfriend. He was new to town, had a car, and was really quiet and nice. We dated for a while. I'd say this was the healthiest relationship I had in my younger years. Not to say he and I didn't try things together. Like drinking, mushrooms, Mary Jane, and ecstasy.

However, we still didn't have a toxic relationship and didn't fight much. We just hit a point where I felt like I was growing, and he wasn't ready to continue growing with me. He struggled in school and to keep a job, and those traits just appealed to me. My father had a fantastic work ethic, and I wouldn't accept anything less than that. We broke up as I was just starting grade ten. Sixteen years old and still living with my uncle.

The night my uncle confronted me about my smoking pot, there wasn't anything unusual about how he asked me to come for a drive with him. Along with babysitting, I also picked up a waitressing job. We stopped to get coffee, and I could sense he had something to say. I figured it would be about my other job—the smell of his thick and musky cologne in the small space of the Honda Civic.

He starts by saying you wouldn't lie to me, would you? Confused, I say, of course not.

"So, when did you start smoking pot?" I shift in my seat, feeling the butterfly swirl around in my stomach. My first thought is, f**k; who would have told him. I decided to be honest and tell him. "Well, I started smoking it when I was 14 to help with my depression. I didn't want to go on medication for it. So, I've been using it to help."

My uncle told me, "That is ridiculous. You know sadness is just a frame of mind, and you just have to change your frame of mind." I'm silent cause that's what I do when I don't agree with someone. I hate confrontation. So, I just go silent. He continues to tell me, “If you want to continue living with me, you'll have to quit. I boldly state well, "I will quit if you quit smoking cigarettes." I don't think he expected that type of response. He sputters that's completely different.

To me, it's not different, and if you think it's so easy to quit, then let's do it together. He doesn't go for it. "The bottom line is you smoke. You can't live with me." So, I go back to my family home.

Some may read this and think I chose drugs over a healthier living situation. And that's a fair assumption. However, it was a medicine for me. Every day was a constant struggle not to want to die.

My best friend hated when I said, "ugh, I just don't care if I live." Sadly, wishing every car that drove past you would actually crash into you, so you could finally be at peace—smiling on the outside but inside feeling as though your stomach is eating itself with worry, shame, and guilt.

Not to mention the worrying. It was so bad by ten years old that I almost gave myself an ulcer. My doctor was so concerned about what she could have to worry about, and my mother said I don't know. She worries about everything. You need to stop doing that. So easy to say, so freaking hard to do. I'd maybe get five hours of sleep at night. I'd lay awake thinking of all the past hurts, replay scenes, and dream of better days. This is what I would carry around just for being me, for existing in this world.

So back to the mountain, and the trailer warmed as the oil furnace roared. Welcoming me back was the smell of cigarettes. It burns my nose. I hate that smell, I thought to myself.

My mother is sitting crossed legged on the bed. Fall time tends to bring out the best in mother. We joke that she goes into hibernation like the bears. Retreating to the dark warm bedroom. Only to emerge for food or to yell at us. Still, I walk for you on eggshells, never really sure what word or action will set her off.

My mother's friend is coming for a visit. I love this friend! Her daughter and I have known each other since kindergarten. She tells me how she wants to go stay with her husband but doesn't feel comfortable leaving her daughter here by herself.

After this summer, I'd be heading to my final year of school. This friend also knows how turbulent my relationship with my mother is. I couldn't be more thankful for her offering me this way out. Of course, this wouldn't stop my mother and me from having another row. A fistfight ended with me shaking, my shirt ripped, and completely done with my mother's shit.

The nasty things she yelled at me still hung in my ears and still creeps in during moments of doubt. "You'll likely end up as a prostitute down in Vancouver. What makes you think you're so special? You think that you are so good because you're going to graduate. It doesn't matter because you are nothing, your worthless trash. You're a stupid little bitch. You're such a disgusting whore." Things a mother should never say to their teen daughter.

The fact that I graduated and didn't manage to kill myself is actually nothing short of a miracle.

The Copper Mountain whore house, I used to call it. The other girls I lived with didn't like the name much, even though most of them were sleeping with other girls' boyfriends. I owned what I was at the time.

Completely in survival mode, working, attending school, and partying just as hard. Showing up to school hungover or still messed up from whatever drug I had taken the night before. Yet I still managed to pass all my classes, some with good grades. I've always had this drive to work hard and succeed, or maybe I was just trying to prove my mother wrong.

Growing up, I wasn't very pretty, yet when I hit my last high school year, I had a glow-up.

Which wasn't such a great thing for me. I was getting all the attention in all the wrong places, hurting my body and heart. At this time in my life, I became very distant from my family. I was mostly cutting all of them out of my life.

On my path of self-destruction. It's tough to tell the difference between love and lust. To all the boys I thought I loved, I'm so sorry I didn't love you. I was hurting and wanting so badly to feel loved. Yet what I should have been striving for was loving myself. The amount of hurt and pain I caused or was caused to me is just gross.

My graduation should have been a fun, easy time. However, I was completely freaking out about my mother. I hadn't really seen her since we came to blows so many months ago. My sister was calling because I was late showing up to the ceremony. We had been drinking out at the lake. I needed to hurry home to do my hair and grab my cap and gown.

I race up to the school in my black sun fire and jump out. I'm only wearing a bathing suit. A man hollers something from his window. There is a row of houses right across from the school. I don't give him my attention because I'm late! It's busy with happy parents and grads. It's so hot outside I don't bother putting on anything but shorts over my swimsuit. I throw on my gown, and away I go.

I find my parents, grandma, and sister anxiously waiting for me to arrive. I awkwardly hug my mom, not really looking at her. Take some pictures and find the principal. They were giving out extra tickets. We could only get one extra. My grandma was about to offer to bow out when I spoke up. It must have been the beers I had beforehand, or my new I don't give a f**k attitude toward my mother.

I said, "No, grandma, you deserve to watch me graduate. You were the one who helped me all those years with my schoolwork. My mother drops her head and proclaims that her asthma is getting worse, and she needs to leave. At that moment, I took back a little bit of my power. You see, my mother is also a narcissist, and what do they like to do when the attention isn't all on them? Well, they ruin events. We have had countless family events ruined by her. Graduation and dry grad was a magical time with my friends that I'll cherish forever.

I planned to move to Kamloops with my best friend just six months after graduating. She is to attend University, and I just wanted to leave my hometown for the first time in my life. Live somewhere new, almost 19 years old. I was ready for a new chapter.

My chapter there didn't last long. My sister called me crying one day. She told me our parents moved an hour and a half away from her. She wasn't allowed to move with them and had to stay behind with her abusive boyfriend and my schizophrenic brother.

They were only sending her $200.00 a month for food. She was 16 at the time, working as a server and taking care of her horse that she bought with her own money! I was livid. I wanted her to move with me, but her boyfriend wouldn't allow it, and she was so wrapped up in their relationship that she couldn't see how toxic it was. So, I made the hard choice to move back home.

I was sad because I had started to hang out with a guy, I had a crush on in high school. We reconnected because we had both moved to Kamloops around the same time. He was very handsome and quiet. He reminded me of my father. He was also a very hard worker, and I liked that. When I broke the news to him, I was surprised by his answer. He said, "No problem! I'll move back with you. I have to go to camp for work in a few days, but when I'm out for Thanksgiving, I'll meet you there, and you can meet my family."

I moved home and found a place to live, a house with a bunch of friends and my sister safe and happy knowing I was close to help when needed. Not to say that I didn't continue to make poor choices and cheat on my poor boyfriend while he was in camp. It still makes me feel so sick that I did that to him.

I was so excited when he told me he was home from camp. He was drunk and then asked me if I even wanted to see him or if I was busy with some other guy—such a punch to the gut. I dropped my head and said, "no, I was alone." To be honest, I don't think he ever got over that betrayal, and I get that.

Hurt people hurt people, unfortunately. I was in such a world of hurt and pain I was becoming the voice inside my head. The person my mother was trying to will me to become. I longed to be loved and looked for it from all the wrong people. This is where I came to the realization, I can't control myself when I'm drunk. So, I promised him I wouldn't go out and party while he was in camp.

We met up, hung out, and partied hard while he was home, as we always did when we were together. This time it was different, though. I saw him for the person he was in our small town. Maybe that's why he moved in the first place, I question myself. He was slipping into old habits, and I was concerned. I asked him if he thought we should move away again. He responded, "I was thinking the same thing, but we will be fine here." What he meant was no way I would trust you to live in a town where I don't have spies everywhere to keep an eye on you.

On the last day before he left for camp, we stayed at his mom's house. She is lovely and kind. She welcomed me in and told me if I ever needed a place to stay, I was welcome there. There was something about our last interaction that stuck with me. I've always been in tune with my body. And I just had a feeling when it was time for my monthly visitor. I had a pregnancy test ready. I wasn't surprised by the positive test result. I was very calm and called my family doctor to make an appointment to confirm it.

I had already figured out what his response would be when I messaged him in camp. He asked me to get an abortion, and at first, the people pleaser in me told him yes. However, upon further thought, I just had a feeling, which wasn't a bad feeling; more like a calling, and you should always listen to your gut.

So, I respectfully messaged him back and told him that if he didn't want to be in our child's life, he didn't have to; however, I wouldn't be getting an abortion. He said, "Okay, well, if we keep it, you will have to tell my mom. I don't want her to hear it from someone else."

Reading his message gave me a lump in my throat. His mother was lovely. I just didn't know her very well. We had only just met a few months earlier. At that meeting, she asked me When I was planning on having children. The number 27 fell out of my mouth. However, the real truth wasn't that I wasn't being careful when being intimate, as I never really cared if I got pregnant.

It was so dark when we showed up at her house that I thought it was only 6 pm. Up North, it gets dark super early in the Fall. She was surprised but thankful for us to stop by. " Come to the kitchen. I'll make us all tea!"

I was so nervous, and I wasn't sure how to bring it up. Sitting at her breakfast bar, I looked down at the band-aid still in the cuff of my elbow. I blurt out, " I had to get blood work done today." " Oh really, are you okay?" She asked. " Yes, well, I'm just pregnant, so they had to run some tests." A look of shock and happiness rushed over her face. She was so excited to become a grandma!

By the time he had gotten home from camp, he was used to the idea of becoming a dad.

It was surprisingly easy for me to stop drinking and doing drugs as soon as I found out I was pregnant. It's almost as though I needed that push, not that children should be a reason to be born to get you sober. However, I've always had a hard time living for myself so knowing that my life wasn't just going to be about me anymore gave me the courage and strength I needed to want to be the best mom I could be for that child!

My child, I think of her as my lifesaver, a gift blessed to me by the creator. To show me what true selfless love looks and feels like. I didn't know much about being a good parent as I didn't feel like my mother gave me a great example other than how not to be. I had other amazing women role models in my life and men who helped to show me different healthy ways to parent.

However, I still attended parenting classes at our local resource center, drinking up all their knowledge. It felt like a home, and I learned so much. They also offered you a healthy, cost-effective lunch.

At this point, I had my sister join me on this journey to parenthood. Though she was only 17, she was also expecting a baby. She and I had a few other friends who joined us in our baby group. I think the class was something we all needed as we all didn't have the best time growing up, and we all desperately didn't want the same struggles for our babes.

One of my biggest takeaways from our group meeting was when they asked me how I'll show my baby love. At first, I was confused, " umm, well, I'll tell her I love her!" That's good. What else?! "Well, I'm not sure how about bathing her. Did you know that's a way you show love? I know that may seem simple." However, to someone that had such a messed-up view of what love was. This simple way of saying even just doing basic simple tasks for your child shows them how much you love them.

So, I did just that, poured all I did for her and turned it into a loving act. I'm not here to say I was perfect all the time. My trauma would still creep up and out of me in moments of extreme stress. I was also casually talking to my mother over this time. Always saying that I wouldn't allow her to hurt me again and yet having people say things like well, you can choose your friends, not your family. Meaning, she's your mom, so get over it.

One day she was driving my sister and me pregnant back to her house; her ex-sister-in-law had been staying with her. My mother does this thing where she takes on " project people," meaning she likes to try to help people she deems need her advocacy and help. Helping them never seems to last long. They always do something that " triggers" her in a way.

Mother lived a hard life, and much that she told me of her past, I was never really sure what was true or not. The things I know for sure are that she was given up for adoption by her young mother and that she lived a life so sad, and that she had so much struggle.

To this day, she hasn't healed properly from her trauma, and that makes me sad for her. Whenever we ask her to see a therapist, she claims that she could school the therapist and how they could help her. To me, she had a wild soul and never seemed to want to stay in one place. Always on the go and loved to travel around.

During this car ride, my mother told my sister and me that she had to ask her sister-in-law to leave. She started to say a bunch of mean things, as she does when she gets angry. Just imagine someone saying the meanest and vile things to you. That's my mother when she is angry. My sister and I sit quietly in our seats. After years of dealing with her mood swings, be know when to choose to listen and not speak. Mother then states, “I have to ask all of you. Someone stole some weed from our room. Was it you girls?"

My sister and I are immediately taken off guard and on the defensive. "What, no!" we both say. “First off, neither of us has been smoking since we got pregnant. Also, if we were smoking and wanted some, we would ask you for it." My sister angrily said, "Why would you even ask us that?!"

My mother, suddenly so calmly, said, "well, I had to ask everyone what you girls think you're so special. I know it probably wasn't you girls, but you girls know it's okay to do drugs every once in a while. Like me, I do hard drugs once in a blue moon." The words what the f**k fall into my mind when she makes the claim. Mother always seems to like to unburden her mind by making these big statements. Also, I think she was jealous of my sister and me as I knew she could never be fully sober from everything when she was pregnant with all six of her children. She was talking about doing cocaine, I think?!

My sister and I have speculated that the last few years, in high school, my mother was working as a cook, out at our local hot springs and hotel. She lost 180 lbs in a few months. She told everyone it was because she was following the Canadian food guide for healthy living; later, I found out she was using hard drugs with my brother in the camper they had outside the hotel.

We arrive back at the family mountain, my sister and I left her car quickly and went right over to our grandma's, we could sense mother's disposition was changing, and we somehow managed to make it the whole car ride without her kicking us out. We figured it was best not to push it and went across the street to grandma's house—our safe haven.

When my daughter was born, I sadly started drinking again. I didn't know how else to deal with my emotions, and all those years of trauma and living in survival mode were catching up with me. Many years later, I discovered the only way to get through your emotions is to feel them. Until then, I numbed the pain of postpartum depression and the baby daddy that I think secretly hated me. Trying to make me remember how much I had hurt him at the beginning of our relationship; by hurting me with words and actions.

My daughter's dad is young and was hurting himself. He struggled in his own way, and we always seemed to fight when drunk. Or he wouldn't come home till super early the following day. Which I hated the most. I didn't care if he drank but just go home early enough that I'm not up all night worrying if you're okay. Forever the worrier.

I thought I'd love to be a stay-at-home mom since her dad worked in camp and would be gone for months at a time. However, I had this longing to be able to work and make my own income.

There aren't many things in life I can't control. What I can control is my work ethic. I was unsure what to do for a job that wasn't serving. I still had very low self-esteem at this point in my life and didn't think I was capable of doing school very much. Also, the cost of school and finding childcare for my new babe all seemed overwhelming.

My sister was attending a self-paced graduation class that allowed you to be expecting or if you already had children. This class had a daycare close by so the student's children could attend. I had freshly graduated, so I often visited her and my nephew on her lunch break. I loved the vibe of the infant-toddler center, and the staff was super lovely.

Upon one of my visits, an educator mentioned, " have you thought of becoming an early childhood educator?" I confessed that I did always dream of becoming a teacher. She explained that we do the same job and that there is so much more than just watching children and learning during playtime. It's just a lot less schooling! I went home excited, and I just had this gut feeling that I needed to take her advice and look into it further.

After talking with friends and family, everyone seemed to agree that it was a great idea. "You can take your daughter with you to work!" That comment sold me, as I wanted to be able to have still my children close and be able to make money. A week later, I applied for the program at our local college! I decided to take the part-time program that would span over two years. By the end of the two years, I'd hold my certificate in Early Childhood Education.

It's funny to me how life works out like that. All these moments that seem small compile into something so much bigger. Or, as I say, everything happens for a reason. And on this path, I with continue to learn and grow.

My life has been a difficult one thus far. I know that the best is ahead of me. And I will forgive and leave my past where it belongs, in the past. I look forward to a bright future.

NOELLA COTE

...

“IT happened. There is no avoiding it, no forgetting. No running away, or flying, or burying, or hiding.”

Laurie Halse Anderson

8

GENERATIONAL TRAUMA

I REFUSE TO BE ANOTHER STATISTIC

"The only person you are destined to become is the person you decide to be."
Ralph Waldo Emerson

When I was six years old, my stepfather threw an ashtray at my mother's stomach, and she retaliated by breaking his nose. She was taken to jail for assaulting *him* and was only allowed leave on June 22, her due date. She gave birth to my sister the following day via emergency c-section while still in custody. I imagine she was probably alone while handcuffed to a hospital bed.

My mom was 24 years old. My baby sister was her fourth child. The doctors thought my baby sister was going to have brain damage. Hydrocephalus: due to her head swelling from being hit with the ashtray in the womb. The umbilical cord was wrapped around her neck, and her heart stopped beating for a moment. My sister almost died twice before she was born. Once during the assault and once during her venture into this world. They chose her name during a supervised visit in the park a week later.

We were told my mom had to stay in the hospital with the baby. Realistically she was still in prison. My brothers and I were left to our own devices. It wasn't uncommon to be left alone for hours in the 90s. I had no idea where my stepfather was, but he wasn't at home when the cars pulled up. At that time, we lived in a motel in Goldstream, Victoria, BC.

A cop car and what must have been Child Protective Services (CPS) were seen pulling into the motel parking lot. I hadn't seen many people wear suits before that. The suits gave us five minutes to grab anything important to us: like a favorite teddy bear, they said. I was scared I would get in trouble for going with them, but I was a child, and they were adults, so we went.

We were driven deep into the mountains for what seemed like an eternity and finally dropped off at our interim foster home. We were only there for a couple of months, but I cried myself to sleep every night while trying to console my baby brothers. They were only two and three years old at the time and probably cried more than I did. The home was never a calm or even a safe place, but a foster home isn't *your* home. We had no idea how long we would be there, and the uncertainty of the situation only made it worse.

I saw a children's counselor during this span. Her name was Sarah, and I still remember playing with her. It was fun and didn't feel like an interrogation. Something normal. Sarah told my mother I had the mentality and stress of a 40-year-old in a six-year-old's body. I am the oldest daughter out of five children, and the weight on my shoulders has often been too much to bear. Three girls and two boys. I was sacrificed to be a caretaker and a mother from a time before I could understand what that meant.

As soon as my mother was released from prison, we were allowed to live with her again. But we had to live away from my stepfather in a transition home. She took him back too easily. Just like she did many times after that.

Soon after, we all moved back to Winnipeg, the frozen city I was born in. It was easier to escape the heat if we left the province, and we did that time and time again. I don't know for sure how many elementary schools I've been to, but it was more than six.

My stepfather physically and sexually abused me for years. The sexual abuse was a secret I buried deep inside myself until I was eighteen. It started when I was eight. We were living in a farmhouse in Lac Du Bonnet, Manitoba.

I was molested by a man my stepfather called his cousin. He spent the night upstairs in the room next to me and made his way into my bed. I could barely make the words, but after three days of trying to get it out of me, I told my mother what had happened. They both told me the man had been "taken care of," whatever that meant. After that, my stepfather thought it was okay, or more like the damage had already been done.

I didn’t get to grow up with my biological father. My mom was seventeen when she got pregnant with me, and their relationship didn’t last. I felt I didn’t have the right to take away my siblings’ father. I sacrificed my sanity to live with my abuser so they would have their father. I couldn't explain any of that to them until later in life.

When they called me their half-sister, and he called me his stepchild, I was destroyed inside. They were my family, and I was loyal to a fault. All I ever wanted was to be loved and accepted. I always had to put on a show so nobody would suspect what was happening. I'm sure some of them still don't understand the war inside my head when we were kids. I didn't think he would do anything like that to his "real" children. He did abuse other girls after me, and you wish you could go back and stop it before it happened to anyone else. That guilt is the heaviest load you'll ever have to carry.

My stepfather had been a part of my life since I was two years old. I wished on every birthday candle that my biological dad would come and take me away. It saddens me to think of how many wishes I wasted on him.

Home felt like a prison I was sentenced to but had no release date. He tried to raise us under the guise of many religions. My mother wasn’t religious, but you couldn’t go against him. We were expected to be very moral and devout, but he was a walking contradiction. The church was more of an excuse to get free food and a reason not to celebrate Christmas. We only didn't celebrate one year while we were Jehovah's Witnesses, but I've never forgiven my mom for that. I had to sit outside the classroom while everyone else sang Christmas carols.

The following year we were Mormon. It was like whoever knocked on the door, and we let them in. I wasn't allowed any friends, especially boys. If you had friends outside the home, that meant he didn't have control over what you did or said in front of other people. You weren't allowed to have fun or joke around; it was all about discipline and control. The moment you acted different than what he expected of you, he knocked you off your feet. I knew what the belt and a backhand were, among other punishments.

When I was ten, I stayed at my maternal grandma's house, where she read my diary. I always had a diary; it was the only way I could vent some of the madness inside of me. The submission she read was that he performed a sexual act on me while I was restrained to the seat of our vehicle. I was supposed to be helping him deliver the Winnipeg Sun newspaper during the summer of 1999. It was impossible for a ten-year-old girl to fight off a grown man, but I felt that was somehow my fault. My grandma quickly informed CPS of what she had read.

CPS showed up at our door. I had to interview with numerous children's counselors and social workers. "Show us where he touched you on the bear." The whole bit. He failed three lie detector tests, but those don't hold up in court. I didn't want to have to face him in court. I was terrified of what he would do to me if he got away with it.

I lay in bed and cried for a week as my mom tried to get me to tell her if it was true or not. All I could do was deny everything; all she could do was believe her daughter. I was so afraid of him, and I didn't want my siblings to hate me for taking their dad away.

I used to pray to Jesus every night that he would get cancer and die so I wouldn't have to look at him anymore. I think the fact that he's still here is the reason I'm no longer religious. To this day, he's never had any consequences for his actions. That was the year I started cutting myself; to feel something other than numb.

A couple of weeks later, we were packed into a van in the middle of the night with whatever we could fit, and we left the province. They picked me up in the middle of my Honor Choir performance, which they didn't attend to watch me sing. They just scooped me up, crammed me in the van, and off we went. This was the first time I went to the same school for more than a year, and I was devastated.

He disowned me for spilling our secret, even though I denied it to my own mother. He never treated me like his child anyway. He treated me like his girlfriend. He was now the talk of the neighborhood, and no one wanted him near their kids or the school, and he hated me for it. I was pleased he got to feel some of the embarrassment and shame I would walk around with for the rest of my life, even if it were only a fraction.

When my mom finally kicked him out for good, we lived in Chilliwack, BC. She didn't leave him because of what may or may not have happened to me; she got tired of the abuse too. We burned everything he left at the house in the fireplace one night, just her and me. He had this big wooden sign of his last name that a friend had made for him. He loved that sign. He hung it on the wall proudly, even though it wasn't mine or my mother's last name. It felt like another small diss to say that I wasn't his real daughter or even a part of his family. I always felt his family name wasn't something you plastered on the wall and were proud of. I rejoiced in burning that most of all. This probably wasn't the best thing to teach your child, but I embraced every ounce of revenge I could get.

After he was gone, you would think things would be looking up. Trust me, I thought they would too. I entered grade seven in 2003. Grade seven. What a time to be alive. It was the end of the year field trip to the Pacific National Exhibition (PNE) in Vancouver, BC. On this morning, my mother and her new man were in the middle of a very loud and violent argument. I threw a TV at his head in her defense. Just before I left the house, he pushed my mom down the front five steps of our house backward, and she landed on her heel on the cement walkway. She lay there damaged on the ground screaming, "IT'S BROKEN!". He laughed at her and told her it couldn't be broken.

You don't really know agony until you hear your mother scream like that. I asked her if she wanted me to call the cops or an ambulance and wait with her. She just told me not to cry or worry about her. Go to school and try to forget because she didn't want me to miss my field trip. That was her way. She always tried to be strong for us. It must have been hard to be strong for herself. I walked to school with my heart shattered into a million pieces and the baggage of leaving her there on the pavement.

My stepfather was waiting two blocks down the road for no other reason than to pry into the situation. He crept around our house regularly. The whole neighborhood could hear what was going on at our home. He asked what happened; I told him. He gave me twenty bucks for my field trip.

I denied what happened to me, so I did have to interact with my stepfather as if nothing had happened for many years. I even had to go for visits with my abuser and the rest of my siblings. It lost all seriousness as time passed, and it damaged me. Even when I eventually told my mom at eighteen, she would talk about it as some archaic thing that happened.

As a mother, I would question what made me come up with the story in the first place. I wouldn't fully believe my daughter's denial, no matter how convincing she might be. There were signs. I would do anything for my mother and my family, but it never felt like they'd do the same for me. You start to wonder if they knew, and you start to resent them.

My mother was in a wheelchair for months. The extent of her injury was so bad they had to fly in a specialist from Toronto to rebuild her heel with plates and screws in the hope that she would walk again. She eventually did walk, but she was never the same.

She can’t stand for long hours. Any hope of gaining employment went out the window.

We now bounced around at friends’ houses, and her ex-boyfriend would follow. His stalking was more persistent and sinister than my stepfather's. One time he melted a concoction of items together into a block of wax and left it on our friends’ doorstep. My mother had a friend who was murdered in Vancouver. She had his zippo lighter from the funeral as a token of remembrance. The zippo was smashed and melted into the wax, along with pills, condoms, and other things, to imply she was a tramp. He did everything he could to rub salt in an already salty wound. We ended up in another transition house, but Chilliwack isn’t very big, and it was no secret which house it was.

When I was in high school, she met a man who had the same birthday as her. It was a whirlwind romance sent from the stars (heavy on the sarcasm). He was around for years, and some of my siblings even considered him a father figure. They were all just my mom’s boyfriends to me. He was there when I graduated. He was in the hospital room when I gave birth. He was a big part of our lives, but just like the others, they would fight. The fights would sometimes turn to violence. I didn’t hate him at first. It wasn’t until after they broke up, we found out he liked little kids too.

I came home from working late at the hotel one night, and as soon as I stepped in the door, I got a phone call from my mom, saying she was hiding in the bushes from the cops, and I needed to come to get her. Being the devoted daughter I am, I went to find her. I still didn't have all the details as to why she was hiding in a bush. Imagine stepping in the door from work and you have your own child, your mom calls you, and you must go. You can't say no.

I pulled up to her apartment, and there were police cars outside. I was entering the building at the same time as two officers. I stepped into the elevator with them and tried to act casual. I made some nervous jokes like, "I bet I know what apartment you're headed to." They looked at me, puzzled. I told them I was her daughter and was coming to see if she was okay. The cops said they were after my mom, not him. Her boyfriend had recently undergone hip surgery. He was living off her, making her care for him, and still treated her like garbage. She took one of his crutches and smashed the windshield of his truck.

I don't think my mother knows how to have a relationship without trauma. I was that way, too, for a time—too much quiet. Too much peace was an imbalance in my hectic existence. I needed the adrenaline to stay interested. I often woke up to screaming and things being thrown. I come from a house with five children. There was always noise, always people. Even now, I must tell myself that calm and peace are what I have been working towards all along. But for some reason, the silence still feels like a loss.

I had it drilled into my brain my whole life not to follow in my mother's footsteps and not to have a child young. I've had a job since I was fourteen years old. There wasn't much to go around growing up. I learned at a young age if you wanted something, you had to work for it yourself.

I partook in my fair share of experimental drugs and drinking in my teen years, but I always got good marks in school. School was my escape from home. It was my safe place. At school, people said you were doing a good job. You were important. Most of all, people said they were proud of you.

I graduated high school only months before discovering I was pregnant at eighteen. It felt like every hope and dream I had for my future was delayed for the next eighteen years. I disappointed my mother, especially myself, and I didn't know how to deal with it for a long time. Everything that happened in my life felt like another curveball I couldn’t handle. Someone kept laying down brick after brick upon my shoulders, and it wasn't fair. Life isn't fair, nor does it owe you anything. Life is whatever you make of it.

My child's father showed red flags from the beginning. There were many signs I should have seen, but I was blinded by teenage love. We were only together a year before I got pregnant. He wanted to keep the baby more than I did. We had our own apartment now, but he could barely hold a job.

As time went on, it got worse. Drinking. Gambling. Drugs. Those were only some of his addictions. Slowly, in my head, I started comparing him to my stepfather. He never took care of his family. The main thing that reminded me of him was his short temper. I was tired of crying and being yelled at for things out of my control.

I was run down by drunken arguments and abuse he didn’t remember. I knew there was a good person somewhere in there; I loved that person. I knew he wouldn’t do half the things he did while he was sober, but the alcohol took over. I felt small and trapped in the body of that eight-year-old girl who couldn’t defend herself.

I was constantly overwhelmed and suffocating. He lost his job mere weeks before my due date, and I didn't qualify for maternity leave. At nineteen years old, I had to figure out what I would do for myself and my son.

We separated for a little while. I couldn't support an extra child and deal with my depression at the same time. My mom was watching my son for me while I worked. Daycare wasn't a thought when my mom was home all day.

My siblings and I started noticing some things about mom. She would disappear for hours or days at a time with no warning. She would borrow my vehicle and, knowing I had to work, arrive late. She was starting to be less of my mother and more of my child. You also couldn't tell her "no." We found a crack pipe in her car, and she tried to blame it on my brother. She crashed her car, which had been a gift from a very generous friend.

At work, I got a phone call that my son was crawling around my mom's apartment by himself, and I needed to get there before CPS did. That's when I lost a lot of respect for her. She used to try when we were younger, but suddenly, she decided to throw in the towel. I needed a mother I could rely on.

When I pulled up, she was fighting with my brother, who was also on hard drugs. She claimed he hit her in the head with a 2x4 piece of wood. They were on the lawn of her apartment building, and there were cops outside. In her craze, she didn't realize she had left her one-year-old grandchild alone in her apartment. I didn't listen to what she had to say. I ran inside with tears streaming down my face, grabbed my son, and left. That was the last time grandma was responsible for him, and I'm sure it killed her.

I bought my child's father a bus ticket to Edmonton, Alberta, on Christmas Eve that year. We had a friend who lived there and sent him with the intention of getting a job since he couldn't hold one down back home. We were still separated. I told him I would consider being a family again if he could get it together. I got my sister to help watch my son while I worked, and in February, I was going to move to Edmonton as well.

Moving across provinces with a child and nothing lined up was scary, to say the least. If he could get a job, I hoped I'd be able to stay home with my son for a couple of months, and things would start to get better. Sometimes you need to change your environment to change your future. Leaving my family behind was one of the hardest things I've ever had to do.

My boyfriend's dad was going to drive out to Edmonton with us and help us move. My mom was supposed to come with us for the drive. My boyfriend couldn't even manage to rent a place for us before we arrived. He was still sleeping on his friend's couch. I had to rent a home from BC, and not many people are willing to rent sight unseen. Luckily things worked out for us, and I managed to rent an apartment with the help of a damage deposit from his parents.

The day we left was the day we had to make it clear that my mom wasn't allowed to come anymore, not after the incident with my son. As I was leaving, she stood in front of my place, and I watched her crumble in the parking lot.

I kept everything together for my mom; without me there, I wasn't sure what would happen to my family. I told her she still had two teen girls to raise. My closest brother was actively in addiction. My other brother split to go live with his father. My youngest sister was only 12 at the time. I told her she needed to focus on being a mom to my sisters and that I was grown now and would be okay. Still, she crumbled. I knew she wouldn't be okay, but I had to get out of that town and give my son a real chance. He deserved something different than the circus that was my life.

Just as I feared, my mom went into a downward spiral. It's difficult watching your mother go through drug addiction. I compare it to mourning someone who's still alive, and that pain will slowly eat away at you if you let it. I wonder every day when I will get the phone call that she isn't here anymore. She injects heroin, smokes crack, and probably does whatever she can get her hands on.

My baby sister witnessed her overdose. I went to see her a month ago for the first time in years. She's still my mom. She's just different now. I had a trauma bond with her growing up and still feel like I've lost a huge part of myself. I may be an adult, but I desperately want and need a mom.

Now I wait for the impending doom that's bound to happen. It took me a long time to realize I couldn't help her. The only person who can help her is herself. I feel guilty for leaving. I think her demise is because of me, but I know that's not on me. She had too many kids at too young of an age and went overboard trying to feel free.

I drove to Edmonton in February of 2011 on the heels of a blizzard. My boyfriend's dad wanted to try and make it back to Chilliwack before the storm. When he drove home, it was so snowy that he could barely see. I was dropped off at the apartment and helped move everything in quickly. We didn't bring much with us, just our mattresses and clothes.

I sat in the middle of my new living room floor and looked out at the snow. I was now in Edmonton, alone with my child. My boyfriend was working out of town building cell phone towers. He wasn't even there to greet us. I knew one person in Edmonton, and he was often working too. The gravity of what I had just decided to do was falling around me. I became depressed and started drinking again.

The plan was to take at least a couple of months off work so I could be home with my son. I didn't have anything lined up, so I went with the flow. I have never expected or wanted a man to take care of me financially, but I desperately needed a moment to focus on being a mom and getting my head back together.

That lasted all of two months. The rent and electricity weren't being paid, and we hardly had the money for food. My son's father was spending the money he made on women and drugs on the road.

Growing up on welfare, I knew what that struggle was, but I didn't want that for my son. I was stressed. My son asked me when he was small if we would ever be homeless. It broke my heart. I promised him he would never need to worry about having a roof over his head or food in his stomach. I would never let him go without those things, which were adult things to worry about. I spent too many years worrying about adult situations I wasn't about to solve as a child.

I got a job at a liquor store far from where I lived. It wasn't by choice. It's what became available. I was only making minimum wage, but I was happy to have my own income again. I didn't have a vehicle anymore due to my 1996 Jeep Cherokee not surviving the Edmonton winter. The winter I spent taking the bus and poor with a toddler was one of the hardest I've experienced.

I had to take the bus for over an hour to work and back. There was a daycare right across from my apartment, and luckily, I was able to get him a spot. I could only work a six-hour shift because I had to get my son from daycare on time. Things started to fall into place even though I was struggling. I began to get depressed because of the time I was spending commuting back and forth. That wasn't my Edmonton dream.

My son's father and I split for good when my son was five. We were engaged, and a series of events led to me calling off the wedding. I couldn't go back to being boyfriend and girlfriend and knew staying with him wouldn't progress me to where I wanted in life. Leaving him was difficult for me as well. I didn't have a child with the intention of raising him in a broken home. I felt like I was failing my son. I always said that when I had control over my own life, it wouldn't be how I grew up.

My boyfriend was drunk one night and threw a fan at my head. The cops came. The cop sat with me, looked me in the eye, and said, "It doesn't get any better. If you don't leave now, you will keep coming back, and who knows where you will end up." That was the soundest advice anyone had really given me, and I took it to heart. I left even though it killed me. I still loved him; I just didn't love what he had become.

As a secretary, I got a job closer to home at a small powersports place. Their parts person was let go, and they asked me if I wanted to try working the parts counter. We only sold aftermarket parts, so it wasn't hard to pick up. You looked in a catalog, and if we could get it, we ordered it in. When I started, I had no knowledge of an engine at all. I didn't know how to change my own oil or a tire. I just kept working my way up. I moved onto a more significant powersports place where I stayed for four years.

I wanted to go to school, but most small outfits didn't want me progressing to the point that I wanted to leave them. Parts Technician is a sought-after trade in Alberta. We have NAIT, a leading polytechnic school in Canada. My employer agreed to let me go to school, but I had to jump through some hoops to get there.

You need a journeyman to sign off on your hours in trade school, but you didn't need a ticket to work in the trade. My employer didn't have any ticketed journeymen working there. I called Apprenticeship and Industry Training, and they agreed that if my employer had sufficient experience in the trade, he could sign off on my hours. I was ecstatic.

One of my dreams had always been to go to post-secondary education. As I said before, I loved school. I love learning. Trade school is only a couple weeks a year, so it was also doable with a child. I completed my first two years at the powersports place, but I wanted to make money. With a Journeyman ticket, I could make upwards of $40 dollars an hour, and that was a success I could never imagine for myself, being a young mother.

That job was like family to me for four years. It was very difficult to say goodbye, but I knew this was my goal. I had to break into the heavy-duty industry to get to the level I wanted. I completed my final year of school at a Caterpillar dealer. I was making more money than I ever thought possible for myself. I cried when I first went to the pharmacy, and my prescription was fully covered because of my health benefits. Coming from where I started, I never imagined I would be here.

Fast forward a few years later, and I am happily married to my best friend. He was someone who saw all my flaws and never doubted wanting me; all of me. He's also the only man I ever dated who kept his word and changed for the better if it was necessary. My son has grown into a wonderful young man.

As soon as his father and I split, he wasn't very involved in his life anymore. It always seemed to be about me and never the son he wanted. He moved back to Chilliwack, and I stayed in Edmonton. My son used to ask why his dad didn't love him anymore. I'm glad he stopped asking. I still feel remorse for leaving that situation, but I wouldn't be where I am today if I hadn't. My son's father recently took his own life.

I carry so much guilt in my life that sometimes it feels like I'm engulfed in misery, even though I have everything I want. My husband is the best father figure to my son I could have asked for. I'm glad he learns what it's like growing up with a dad, especially one he's not afraid of.

I have a career and the family I longed for all those years. I constructed all of this for myself. I wasn't going to lay down and become another statistic of generational trauma. I must tell myself to be proud. I can't wait for my mother to tell me. I still feel lost sometimes, and the loneliness can be unimaginable, but I face my demons head-on every day.

We have the power within ourselves to change our stars, and we must believe we can get there.

TESSA WHITE

...

"At some point, you just gotta forgive the past, your happiness hinges on it."

Aaron Lauritsen

9

EMPOWERMENT

COMES WHEN WE LET GO

"I always get to where I'm going,
by walking away from where I've been." Pooh

When I was a child, I learned about instability. I learned that as a child you can become accustomed to patterns of behavior in the world that catch you off guard if they shift. When things in my young life were uncertain, it encouraged me to build a protective wall in case other unexpected things happened, like changing schools again and again or moving to another apartment building again and again and again.

It took me a long time to learn how to be comfortable in stillness or feel safe enough to trust someone with my heart. When someone is in charge of looking after you and they can't for whatever reason, I think it makes us second guess the capability of others... maybe even ourselves for trusting them in the first place. For many years I didn't trust myself to become a mother based on my lived experience.

I grew up in poverty in East Vancouver. When I was nine years old, my stepdad left my mom, my brother, and I, and with the single income also gone, we ended up on welfare and using food banks. Clothes were second-hand, and Christmas was full of second-hand books and mom's tears.

I remember one Easter when a bag of chocolate treats were left outside our apartment door from an unknown source. My mom was so thrilled, she hid them around the apartment, and we had an Easter egg hunt.

Between the ages of 9 - 12, I watched my mom struggle to give us the best life she could despite her own history of childhood abuse and despite the fact that she didn't have a license or a job. I know she tried her best and loved us.

"Mom, why are you in a weird mood?" I would ask. As a child, I was confused about why my mom wanted to rearrange the furniture at 1:00 am on a school night. I mean, everyone is a little weird, in my opinion, and the best ones usually are, but when I would awaken to Beach Boys or Alanna Myles blasting in the middle of the night, I was frustrated, tired, and sometimes scolded by mom for not being 'more fun.'

It wasn't until I was a teenager that I realized all those late evenings of dancing or home decor creativity were actually because my mom was tipsy. Sometimes we would argue so loud about her being noisy that the neighbors would call it in. We had social workers visit us months before I voluntarily moved out.

Are you familiar with the dried butterfly decorations in those glass frames? My mom had about 20 of them hung up on the living room wall of our house. They were there during all the disorderly evenings. They were there during all the embarrassing pre-teen moments in front of my friends. They were there during all our arguments.

It took several years after leaving that house for me to realize the association that caused me to shudder at the sight of them as I do with spiders. Fortunately, with difficult situations and emotions, it's all temporary. I now have a glass butterfly hanging on the wall in my kitchen as an intentional move toward personal growth. It's an identical specimen to the one my mother had, and now I can appreciate its beauty.

Turning Points

I was learning that my mom prioritized fun over keeping a quiet night time environment, and it frustrated the hell out of me. Was it every night? No, not at all, but when I look back on the last year, I lived with her it's what I recall most. Eventually, her fun evenings became fun days, leading to some awkward interactions with my already awkward pre-teen buddies and me. My little brother didn't seem phased by it, though, and why would he? Being a little boy with a super fun mom who always wanted to have fun was like winning the kiddo lottery… for him.

Once I turned 12 years old, I started sneaking my mom's pink fizzy drinks from the fridge. Naturally, a healthy child goes through the motions without overthinking it, but I was starting to second guess what I was experiencing, and I felt confused.

Mom's daytime tipsies continued to intensify until I was unable to confide in my mom about teenage girl drama and was picking up/ dropping off my little brother from school independently. I had always felt close to my mom as a child and could tell her anything, but when my teenage hormones kicked in, and her tipsies were revved up, we started to clash. Taking a note to the store to buy her smokes up on Hastings didn't feel like a cool thing to do anymore, but more of a nuisance.

Some of these arguments turned physical and led me to confide in my friends, their parents, and, eventually, my school counselor. I remember one argument in particular about my boyfriend, my first boyfriend. He came over to our house one evening to watch a movie and play a board game in the living room. My mom joined us, wearing shorts and a tank top with her hair in two braids. At the time, she was over 300 pounds, and I felt very embarrassed by how she looked. The fact that knew she was tipsy also bothered me. I just wanted the night to be over.

Situations flooded over to my Catholic school too. My mom had joked with me about how cute my grade four teacher was, but I never imagined she would act on it. One day she came to pick me up from school and told me to wait in the hall outside my classroom. I looked in and could see him sitting at his desk, and there she was, bent over it with her face close to his courting him. They never went out, but I was completely mortified.

I remember another time after choir practice. She cried to my choir leader about our financial situation and how next year I would be in public school. I sat on the altar of the church while she cried to the director in the pew, who could do nothing but listen. I knew these things were not 'normal' mom behavior, but I didn't think I had any family or healthy friends' moms to confide in.

When I was 12 years old, a dear friend at school wrote me a private letter the last week I lived in my mom's care, explaining that she was experiencing suicidal ideation. My mom read the letter, and I believe what transpired next bled out of her fear and concern for me.

That final evening in my own house, my mom came into my bedroom while I was doing homework and demanded that I no longer associate with this friend, that I stay away from her, and that she would be calling my friend's mom to tell her about the letter. When I protested, she put her hand around my neck, and with her face inches from mine, she whispered, "What are you going to do? Stab me with your pencil?" Stunned, I dropped the pencil. "Now go have a shower and get over it."

Deciding

Fight or flight. I went into the washroom, diary in hand. With the door locked and the shower on, I cried my eyes out on the washroom floor, hugging my knees and silently bawling my eyes out. I journaled everything in my diary out of fear that I would forget something (many of my childhood memories faded from early stress).

When I was finished, I wet my hair to make it look like I'd had a shower, and I went back to my room, journal hidden in my clothes. That night as I lay in my bed for the last time serenaded by Black Velvet, I made a decision. My hyper-emotional and exhausted 12-year-old mind and heart knew I had to share this with another adult, one I trusted who would be sober and safe.

That next day at school, I went straight to my school counselor's office in the morning and told her everything. After my disclosure, I said, "Now, one of two things is going to happen. If you tell my mom I talked to you, she's going to be really mad, and I'm not going home. If you don't tell her, I promise I'll keep coming to talk to you, and you can help me deal with this." She explained that legally she was obligated to report this to the Ministry of Child and Family Development (MCFD). "Then I'm not going home tonight." I never stepped foot in my house again.

That day I was in and out of classes, being paged to the counselor's office on and off to answer questions while she worked through her reporting processes. "Kate, you don't have to go home tonight. We have a safe place for you to stay." I knew my mom was going to be pissed! I was grounded after the altercation from the previous night and thought she might show up at my school if this took much time after classes were over.

At 3:30 pm I was still working through things with the counselor in her office when a roar came from the front reception, "WHERE is my daughter!" Heart pounding. A hot red flush took over my body, and my counselor's wild eyes struck even more fear into me, "Kate, stay here." Palms sweating. She left and closed the door behind her. I grabbed my hair. I made fists. I paced alone in that office, wondering what to do. *What have I done? Oh my god, this is a mistake.*

I heard mom yelling in that all too familiar tone and thunderous voice, directing her rage at the receptionist and counselor. I peeked out the tall narrow window in the office door and saw her through the metal wires on the glass, grateful they were there. She was disheveled and in a fury. I locked the office door and hid underneath the counselor's desk.

Running

Head spinning. There I was, huddled under the office desk hugging my knees and rocking to self-soothe. "I'm okay. I'm okay." I looked at the window behind me and considered stepping out onto the ground. After a few minutes of listening to my mom yell at the school staff, the counselor knocked on the door, "Kate, it's me."

I slowly and shakily crawled to the door and looked at her through the window. With our eyes locked, she quietly said, "Kate, a social worker is here and is going to take you to a safe place to stay tonight. Your mom has been drinking and is very upset, so we need to wait for the police before we can get you out." I nodded and returned to my safe spot under the desk.

"Oh F**K no. F**K YOU," my mom's alert that the police had arrived. The route for me to exit the office and get outside consisted of a long hallway where the police were holding my mother's arms. "Kate, it's time to go. I'm going to walk in front of you, and this officer will be behind you. We're going to be walking past your mother in the hallway. You will be safe. The social worker will meet you outside, and I will walk you to her car." I nodded.

There were no words for what I was experiencing. Looking back now, I felt fear and guilt, and like my mother and I had each betrayed the other. I stepped out of the office behind the counselor, in front of the cop, and with haste, I was escorted past my mother, who stood to my left, held back by two police officers. She never looked up at me. She just stared at the floor. I felt so terrible for her. What had I done?

But if the police, social workers, and my school counselor all agree it is best for me to leave my mom, did that mean it was the right thing to do? From that moment on, I was legally under the guardianship of the Province of British Columbia and never went back into her care despite all our best efforts to reconcile over the next several years.

The social worker appeared to be about 25 years old and drove a red sports car; being an impressionable pre-teen, I was surprised and somewhat excited. She seemed more like a cool big sister than a professional. “Okay, Kate, this is where I leave you. We’ll talk again when you return to school. It will be all right. You did the right thing.” The counselor opened the car door and without anymore time to reconsider, I stepped into the sports car and left with the social worker.

She seemed nice, young but nice. My house was a 10-minute walk from my school… “Kate, I understand your little brother is at home alone, so we’re going to pick him up.” I was thrilled with this news! We drove off the school lot and arrived at my house,

“You cannot open the door because you’re no longer in your mother’s care. It would be a break-and-enter. All we can do is knock and wait for him to answer the door and come with us willingly.” I knocked. Nothing. Heart pounding with excitement. I knocked again. No answer. I was banging and yelling for him, but no one came.

Suddenly, my mother approached from behind us, “Get the hell off my property. You don’t live here anymore.” The social worker grabbed my arm, “Kate, go get in the car now,” I ran. From inside the car, I watched as my mom threw choice words at the social worker, who soon returned to the seat beside me.

As we were pulling away with my mom watching us, my six-year-old brother, who was home alone, opened the door to the house. I made eye contact with him. So close. I still shake my head when I think about how life would have been so different for us had he come down one minute sooner.

She drove me to her parent’s house. In East Vancouver, there are alleyways to most of the houses, and people use them as often as the sidewalks. We drove down an alley, and she stepped out of the car without turning it off. She yelled up to the back deck of a house where people were having a BBQ and having a conversation in another language. She was telling them she couldn't make the family dinner. Instead, she took me for nachos at Cactus Club, I remember thinking she was really pretty, and I wanted to be just like her when I grew up. Free-spirited, bilingual so she must be so smart, pretty, cool car, saving kids and going for nachos - my hero.

After dinner, we went to a hotel room for the night. It had two single beds and smelled like cigarettes, but I didn't care. By this point, I was feeling empowered, independent, and relieved. I was the one who did this. In my lost state, I was letting go of the emotions that used to consume me, and I was exhausted.

At twelve years old, in a lost hotel room with a stranger, I began to understand that my uncertain young mind could be still. In this stillness, I began to find myself, and I promised myself I would be my own best friend forever because no one is ever going to know exactly what I'm thinking and feeling except me. My heart relaxed as I accepted that the desire for something else in life is okay to want and even better to act on.

Moving

The next day I was moved into a group home with other kids recently removed from care. Still located in East Vancouver, I only had contact with my mom and brother over the phone, most often with the conversations ending with ferocious power struggles. "NO, you can't have any clothes. You can have your shit when you come home!" All my mom gave the social workers for me were two garbage bags of my stuffed animals. It was autumn, and I was longing for my comfy sweater. And mom snuggles.

The kids in the group home were abrasive, to put it mildly, they'd steal my make up and I'd steal it back, then we'd share a smoke. With these new comrades, I was exposed to all sorts of dangerous situations. One evening a girl who lived in the house invited me out to meet a couple of guys. During that outing, my first kiss involved being pushed up against a wall with some guy's tongue in my mouth, I was frightened, and it was easier to go with it than say no.

I witnessed my first hate crime (racial slurs thrown by 'our guys' that night at some black kids on the city bus). I broke the law (damaged public property) and broke curfew. It was confusing to know which house rules to follow when some of the staff illegally bought smokes for the youth and others encouraged homework. Chaos. Looking back now, I can see how youth living in these environments can so easily develop massive attitudes toward authority and spiral downwards instead of up.

As winter approached, my mom was offered an investment opportunity to join in opening a franchise restaurant on Vancouver Island, so she moved to a small town outside of Nanaimo with my brother. "Well, Kate, if you want a shot at moving back home with your mom and brother, you'll need to follow them out to the Island. We found a foster home for you in the next town over from your mom's new rental."

I had a phone call and then a visit with my soon-to-be new foster mom. After telling me, she was gay, I quickly replied, "Oh, that's cool. I've never really had a dad around anyways, and I can handle chicks." She laughed, and we hit it off. In November of 2000, I moved away from East Vancouver to her home in a small town on Vancouver Island.

. . .

Fostering

My experience in foster care was nothing short of miraculous. The family I moved in with consisted of a mother, her biological daughter, who was two years younger than me, her biological son, who was the same age as my brother, and two cats. It was a warm family home within walking distance of the ocean and a 50-acre bird estuary.

Nature became the core of my spirituality, grounding me to this day are dirt paths and trips on or near the water. When I was a young child, I used to walk up to trees, hug them and thank them for the air, so this naturalistic environment felt very home-like to me right away.

My foster family expanded to cousins, grandparents, aunts and uncles, and even more people abroad. The entire family was always kind to me, even when I struggled.

My teenage years were a mixed bag of volunteering with the local community center, playing school sports, and rebelling by breaking curfew and hanging out with the 'wrong crowd.' I was dating the baddest boy in town while also volunteering to organize Easter on Ice for children at the local arena.

I must credit the tough love from my foster mom. She took no shit from me and always pushed me in the right direction, whether I was being bitchy or warm. She enrolled me in volunteering with Leaders in Training in the community, and I stayed with the group for a few years until I started playing school sports which she also pushed on me to keep me out of trouble.

She worked at my high school, and one fine day she busted me for smoking weed during class. I remember her marching me to the principal's office and asking that I be suspended! I spent that week doing so much weeding of her property as a punishment. I could have died. Ironically enough, I now love gardening. Funny trick there, life.

Since the school suspension was drug related, I was kicked off the rugby team. I remember going up to the coach once I returned and telling him how important staying on the team was for me, that it kept me in a safe place rather than with the wrong crowd I'd fallen into. And the next day, I was back on the team. I apologized to my mates and that that was the end of it. I emailed him a couple of years back to thank him again, he in turn applauded my life choices yet again, and said it made his year to hear I was doing well.

Although the love was always strong between my foster sister and I, when I was deep in the throes of teenage rule breaking, we went for over a year without speaking a word to one another. We went from catching giant west coast spiders in cups, running through the backyard woods, and having midnight games of Crazy Eights that lasted hours or even days, to silence.

It wasn't just chilly, it was nothing. I remember feeling our frustration with each other. Today she is one of my best friends and godmother to my child, which just goes to show how strong family bonds are regardless of biology. My foster mom, grandma, aunt, uncle, and cousin have all lived in the same town as me, and they will always have a huge part of my heart.

My family consists of my partner's family, my mother, my brother, all of my foster family, and a few close friends I've been blessed with. I appreciate blood relatives and the biology behind family like that, yet I also think it takes a certain level of commitment to maintain family bonds when none were given from birth. I so appreciate these individuals who are determined to stay in my life by choice, not some biological obligation.

Visiting

Visits with Mom after moving away were rough. The first few visits were supervised and often cut short due to our arguing and the social worker calling it. Eventually, we reached a place where we no longer needed supervision during the visits, or so we thought.

During my first Christmas living on Vancouver Island, my foster family went overseas for a family vacation, and I stayed in respite care. During that time, my mom invited me over to her new rental house. The first part of the visit was fairly smooth. She showed me a bedroom that she had all set up for me with lots of new clothes and all my old things, but said I wasn't allowed to have any of it until I moved home.

"Sometimes I come in here and play with your things," said my little brother. I could tell he was trying to annoy me, but I just thought it was cute, and I missed him so much that I didn't care. She also showed me the back deck of the house and boasted about how the floor had heating underneath it. I was picking up on how she wanted me to feel remorse, but all it seemed to do was piss both of us off.

As the visit went on, so did the aggravation between us. As my mom sat across from me in the living room, glaring and sipping that all too familiar pink cider, which caused me to take out my cell phone and called the respite worker to come to pick me up. My mom flipped. I spent the next 15 minutes with my mom standing over me, telling me how I betrayed her and my brother and needed to grow up and stop being such a dramatic little bitch.

I could always tell when she was really pissed because her voice would get really low, and she'd be very physically close to me.

When I heard the knock on the door, I already had my things gathered, and like a wounded fawn, I fumbled my way past her (again), wondering if she was going to grab me. I opened the door, and the respite worker was there, unaware of how tense the situation was. I could see she was very excited to meet my mom and wanted to have a friendly chat. My mom told her off and slammed the door. My brother was yelling in the background that I was a little bitch, unaware of what the words meant. I was withdrawn for the next few days leading up to Christmas.

That was the last time I ever saw my mom in that house. After being swindled out of an investment opportunity to start a restaurant business, she was no longer able to afford rent, and shortly after, she and my brother moved to a small one bedroom suite in the same city as my foster home, but it too was very short-lived.

"You ruined all of my job opportunities. I have a terrible reputation in this town," said my mom, who had now decided she wanted to be a drug and alcohol counselor again. Throughout my entire childhood, I'd never witnessed my mother actually have a job, so I didn't completely take this on as my fault, but I'd be lying if I said I didn't think I made her life worse by leaving her.

After that Christmas, our relationship went from bad to worse, with terrible phone calls ending in fights. "One…" said my mom. "Oh my God, Mom, are you seriously counting to three over the phone?" She had counted to three when I lived with her as a warning for me to stop whatever I was doing *or else*. "Two…" "what the f**k, Mom, this is ridiculous! What are you going to do? Reach through the phone and grab me?" CLICK.

COURT

While my relationship with my mom was deteriorating, I was simultaneously developing strong bonds with the members of my new foster family. "Well, Katie, the six-month temporary placement agreement with the MCFD is going to expire soon, so we need to decide what we're going to do next."

After experiencing the family dynamics with my foster family, complete with scrabble nights, sleepy time tea every night, and serious structure, I decided to attempt a legal permanent placement for me there.

My mom was never going to agree to allow me to move out and live with a foster family permanently until the age of 19. Looking back now as a new mother myself, I can't imagine my child saying in a court of law that she was refusing to live with me. I had to stand in front of a judge in a courtroom and explain why I wanted to live with my foster family instead of my mom and my brother. The ultimate betrayal. The nail in the coffin.

I remember sitting there in the front row next to my foster mother and my biological mother on the other side of the aisle, also in the front row next to my little brother. My mother wouldn't look at me, but my brother kept giving me dirty looks. As an angry 6-year-old, all he knew was that his sister didn't want to live with him anymore, and he was furious with me. He was throwing me angry, dramatic scowls and shaking his head, and waving his finger at me as though I'd been a naughty girl.

I don't remember much about this day, but from what I've read in my files (which I acquired through a Freedom of Information request) and what I've been told from witnesses when I was asked to tell my side of the story, I never had to go up. When I told my story, the judge simply asked me to stand up and share my experience from where I was in the row. The verdict was immediate. I was to live the rest of my days in foster care until adulthood.

My mother left in disbelieving tears with my brother in tow. I left in tears, relieved yet heartbroken. I don't remember what else happened that day or the days that followed. It's a blur.

OVERDOSE

Within two months of the hearing, she and my brother left Vancouver Island and moved back to Vancouver. I remember feeling alone and abandoned even though I actively participated in my removal from her. Sometimes the consequences of our actions are so deep-rooted it takes years to totally process them, and that's okay… I think it's just more difficult for children.

A few years later, while on shift at the local pizza place, I received a call from my social worker. My mother had overdosed on methadone and had no brain activity, "Oh my God, Katie, I can't believe I just told you this over the phone. I'm coming over to you right now." I told my boss I had to leave for a family emergency and stepped out into the parking lot, where I saw my social worker running across to meet me. I fell into her arms and onto my knees.

I thought my mother was going to die that day. My social worker took me back to my foster home, where my foster mother embraced me with tears in her eyes. I didn't know what to do. I felt like I had to do something. I felt like this was my fault. Ever since I left my mother's care, her drinking increased, and she started using heavier drugs. Was this because of me? Had I caused more pain for her and my brother even after I left?

"Katie, if you want to quickly pack an overnight bag, we can get you to the next ferry to go and see your mom." Everything was arranged for me to be picked up on the other side and driven to the hospital. Before I left the house, the last update was that my mother was unconscious with no brain activity, and I learned that my little brother had found her unresponsive in bed. "Katie, you should know your little brother has been removed from your mother's care. He found her unconscious, and after trying to wake her up unsuccessfully by banging pots and pans together near her head, he ran to the neighbor's house (where she had ingested the methadone), and they called 911." Had he not done anything, she would have died that day.

I was driven to the ferry and dropped off, assured that someone would pick me up on the other side. As I sat on the ferry, I thought about the last time I spoke with my mom and the argument we had. I thought about my little brother, and I wondered what he was thinking and how he was feeling. I wondered if he would be able to move in with me on Vancouver Island and if would we be together if my mom died.

What would happen if she died? What would happen if she survived? How would things change? How would things stay the same? What things get worse? Would my brother blame me later in life? Do I blame myself? Is someone actually going to pick me up on the other side? How can I be sure of anything in this life anymore? How can I ever trust another adult? How could I ever be a mother? How did mom do this? Did she mean to do this?

I was picked up by an extended foster family member on the mainland and driven straight to the hospital. "Katie, I have miraculous news, your mother has woken up." Realizing that my mother would survive, I say suddenly became furious at her.

"Your brother is currently with a foster family for now, and we're going to go to the hospital and see your mom if that's what you want to do." I did want to see my mom, but I also wanted to see my brother. I wanted to hold him and tell him it would be okay. I wanted to reassure him that even though we couldn't live with my mom anymore, there were wonderful families out there that could take care of him in a way he'd never understood before. I desperately wanted him to move in with me. But I didn't get to see my brother, not yet.

We arrived at the hospital and parked the car. My heart was beating so fast, and I felt so nervous. We took the elevator up and walked up to a desk with a nurse there. We told them who we were, and we asked where my mother was. The nurse looked at us confused and pointed to my right. I had seen my mom in several months and didn't recognize the person on the gurney five feet away from me.

I stared at her from a distance for about a minute before I approached the side of her bed. Her body had transformed. She lost over 150 pounds since I'd seen her last if I had to guess. She had some marks on her face. Were they scabs? I put my hand on her arm, "Hi, Mom, it's me, mom. Can you hear me?"

Without opening her eyes, she frowned and said, "what are you doing here." My heart broke at that moment. She had been so close to death with no one there for her, yet here I was, and she couldn't accept it. "I was in the neighborhood," went my sass mouth, and with that, she drifted off into sleep, and we left as I choked back some tears.

The next day social workers brought my brother to the hospital parking lot to see me briefly. They explained that since my mother was now awake, my brother would soon be returning to her care.

It turns out that all you need to care for a child is the ability to provide food, clothing, and shelter, which my mother could technically do. When I asked my brother how he was in the foster home, he excitedly told me about their pet dog and his cool room. He was only eight years old and couldn't quite grasp the seriousness of everything that had happened. He was returned to her care two days later… I still shake my head when I think about that.

DIVERGENCE

Over the next several months, my desire to 'party' with my friends and experiment with risky behaviors diminished. I had been 'scared straight,' it would appear. Unfortunately for my brother, my mom was still dabbling in the scene, and soon after the overdose, she lost her housing.

They lived in a few women's shelters until he was 12 years old, like I was when I voluntarily went into care. With the courage of a lion, my brother took the bus to an MCFD office and asked to speak with a social worker. He was also removed from mom's care, also moved into an amazing foster family, and also lived with them for a long time. The two parents were stable and warm, their two children were healthy and played sports in school, they had a golden retriever, and they lived within walking distance of the house my mom squatted in. He was able to visit her whenever he wanted to, visits that became less and less frequent as time went on.

Two things haunt me to this day:

What is rock bottom?

What causes my brother and me to thrive?

I try not to overthink the first question because I believe it is relative to a person's capacity to understand loss, and with my mom's addiction, she constantly focuses on the present moment and shifts away from loss. As I continue to live a healthy, stable, full life, I actively explore the second.

Since my brother and I left, we completely diverged from a path of drug abuse. I pursued careers in social work and government policy while running small hobby businesses on the side, and my brother is a successful member of the Canadian Armed Forces, quickly moving up the ranks. We are close friends, and I couldn't be prouder of him.

ADULTING

My adult relationship with my mom is less volatile than when I was a youth, but it still ebbs and flows. We seem to go through periods of closeness with phone conversations every other week and texts for months without much communication at all.

Since the recent birth of my daughter, we've had more communication than we have over the past decade. However, I still work to consciously maintain boundaries because she is still in the 'lifestyle,' and I refuse to have my child exposed to this as she becomes more aware of her environment. I once visited her with my brother when we were both in care, and she was sleeping in a turned-over shopping cart behind a church. Life is crazy.

I actively work on not feeling guilty about her situation, which has improved over the last three years! Income assistance paid for her training, and she has gained employment working as a flagger for a construction company. I have voiced a strong boundary that we do not discuss her 'use' or drama with people she knows. I just can't take all that in. I won't.

Themes surround my relationship with my mom. I feel a sense of urgency, or maybe it's fear that I will lose her soon. I worry that if I don't make that phone call or try and schedule that visit, I might never get the chance again. Sometimes this fear clashes with my boundaries, and I sacrifice my desire to relax and crochet for a weekend … but is this not selfish? Shouldn't I want to nurture this relationship with her? Isn't it my responsibility to nurture the relationship my daughter has with her grandmother?

Further down the rabbit hole, I have uncertainty with imposter syndrome, wondering at times what exactly I am feeling and what my real intentions are. Am I appeasing an obligatory feeling deep in my biology, or am I actually finding a balance? Shouldn't I know? My brother says she gave up the right to have us in our lives years ago, and my relationship with her is truly a charity, but I don't think so.

I don't think I have found the balance because the last time my mom came to visit my daughter and me, she said, "I feel like an outsider, Kate. Like you only see me out of obligation. I want you to come to visit ME on the mainland, not just see me on your way through to somewhere else."

I understood her and, for a moment, agreed that it was obligatory, but I also know that I love her so much. When we talk, she often has manic moments and rambles about the chaos of her work politics. It aggravates me to the core so that I now find myself annoyed with her eccentric mannerisms, mannerisms she's had my whole life.

In response, "Mom, would it even be realistic for the three of us to come to visit you for dinner and stay overnight?" I didn't even mention our large dog, who travels with us. She looks at the floor. I think the idea of having a closer relationship with me is much different than what the reality of it would look like, and she has a difficult time reconciling this.

She is currently renting a basement bedroom and does not have much privacy or space. "Mom, you told me your place is so messy you won't even have your best friend over. Would you want us to sleep over at your house?" Her answer was, "well, no," and although she didn't say so, I could see she felt shame.

"Kate, I have been very close to cutting you off recently, just shutting this down." Defensiveness. We both feel it when discussions become threatening like this. "I don't know what the right path forward is, Mom, but I know we love each other, and we both want to have a relationship. For now, at least, I think that is enough to keep trying." She nodded.

Experiences like this one in the fall of 2022 remind me to hold my boundaries strong. She can threaten me all she wants, but as I grow into motherhood, I feel a protective nature to safeguard my daughter from this because the emotions I work through, after these encounters could be noticed by her. A crying mommy is not a happy present mommy.

It is disappointing, and it is a loss. A loss of future potential. I can say, "I wish it was like… Maybe if she would … "but the situation is what it is. I will never lose faith in my mom's ability to love me, and I know she is a very strong woman who fights for what she believes in. I do love her, and I do wish things were different, but it makes me teary to wish for things that haven't been and likely won't ever be. "No expectations, ever hopeful," says my mother-in-law.

WHAT I KNOW

I love my mom, and I always will. I love my foster family and always will. Above all else, I am protective of my daughter, and I am forever devoted to my family life with my amazing partner.

Have you ever realized your idea of how life should be is predicated on another person's behavior or the permanence of a relationship? Learning that we can separate our being from some idea of how the world operates is liberating. I am so much more than a daughter or a mother. I am a learner, a creator, an observer, and an interpreter. This life is so precious, and I am grateful every day for what I choose to surround myself with.

I do not consider myself lucky or unlucky, and I believe I have manifested an incredible life to which I credit… myself! Sometimes when life gives you crap, you, fortunately, get a new life.

KATE RITCHIE

...

"The older I get, the more I believe that the greatest kindness is acceptance."

Christina Baker Kline

MEET THE AUTHORS

JUNE PALMER

A REMEMBERING

MEMORIES CARRIED FROM ONE GENERATION TO THE NEXT

June Palmer is a First Nations Iskwew (woman) from Sturgeon Lake Cree Nation in Alberta Canada.

June is married to her sweetheart Brian. June a proud mother of four, a Kohkom (grandmother) to Thorin, Caroline, Marie, Raya and Marceline.

June is an amazing intuitive healer with a passion for sound healing. She travels extensively sharing her sound medicine and intuitive gifts and talents. June's spirit lodge name is Mikwan, which means feather in her Cree language.

You can connect with her on her website www.mikwanenergyworks.com or on social media.

Facebook – Mikwan Energy Works

https://www.facebook.com/mikwanenergyworks

Instagram – Mikwan Energy Works

https://www.instagram.com/mikwanenergyworks/

KATELIN STANVICK

FACING ADVERSITIES

I SEE THE LIGHT, AND IT'S BEAUTIFUL

Katelin was born in Northern British Columbia, in the small town of Terrace, BC. She loves her little town, the warm summers, and the mild winters. Terrace has a natural "greenhouse" effect due to the beautiful Coast Mountains.

She was the third of four children. Throughout Katelin's childhood, she faced her family's addictions and negative behaviors due to alcohol and drug abuse. Katelin lost her mother to addictions when she was twelve, and rather than accepting help that came her way, she rebelled.

Katelin's life has been a search. A search to find love. A search to find a protector. A search to find family. A search to find a home and belonging. Then one day, she woke up and realized, what she was searching for all those years, was right there, inside her.

Giving birth to a beautiful baby girl, Katelin knew it was time to leave the past behind and forge ahead into a new life. As a single parent, she worked incredibly hard and earn her Bachelor's Degree in Social Work at the University of Northern British Columbia. Relying on the charity of others, government assistance, and local food banks, as hard as it was, Katelin never gave up her dream of a better life for herself and her daughter.

Now Katelin helps others who are in similar situations as the family she grew up in. She is a full-time Outreach Worker and a part-time Therapy Assistant. She is proud of her accomplishments thus far in life and always looks forward to a bright future.

If you'd like to reach out to Katelin, this is where you can find her…

Instagram: https://www.instagram.com/_kate.mariie_xo/

Facebook: https://www.facebook.com/katelin.donahuestanvick

LISA KALINSKI

UN-APOLOGETICALLY ME

LIVING WITH ADHD

Lisa spends most of her time on her three true passions in life, writing, teaching, and shopping! And she spends every possible minute outdoors admiring the beauty and walking the trails of her mountain property on Mt Woodside in Agassiz.

Shortly after graduating with a diploma in Travel and Tourism in 1989, she spent her early working years in the tourism industry, first as a bus driver and local tour guide before venturing into long-distance tours throughout Canada and the United States. With her zest for life and travel, she fell easily into the role as host to the local sights and scenery.

In 1993 with nearly a million miles under her belt, teaching quickly became a passion of hers, and she went into the driver training/licensing industry for a decade, which she returned too in 2018. After dabbling in this and that for a few years during slower markets, Lisa started Roundabout Driving School in early 2019, and it is a perfect fit.

In 2002 Lisa took the plunge and entered the Real Estate industry, which had long intrigued her, and she loves to shop with clients. She doesn't have the same stamina for that business full-time anymore, but she still enjoys helping repeat clients and referrals. Not to mention, it keeps her out of the mall 😊. Somewhere along the way, Lisa has developed a real passion for storytelling through writing.

Coming from a family of storytellers, including authors, play rights - and even a TV producer, while taking a hiatus from the Real Estate business, she found herself drawn into the challenge of creating two local neighborhood magazines. Although she didn't write the stories for her magazines at that time, she found it fascinating to learn about people, and the readers really enjoyed learning about their neighbors.

Lisa lives in Agassiz, British Columbia and has a hubby, three kids, three grandkids, two dogs, and a cat.

GUELDA REDMAN

A BROKEN MIND

OUR JOURNEY WITH SEVERE MENTAL ILLNESS

Guelda Redman lives in Chilliwack, British Columbia, on 2 ½ acres with her husband, daughter, and daughter's family. She is an animal lover and keeps alpacas, sheep, goats, and poultry, as well as her dog and cats.

Currently caring for her two sweet grandkids during the weekdays and her 95-year-old mother full-time, life never slows down. But she wouldn't have it any other way.

While navigating a Schizophrenia diagnosis for her son, she also developed severe depression herself. Learning more about mental illness and how it can affect you has been a roller coaster experience, to say the least.

After discovering the British Columbia Schizophrenia Society (BCSS), Guelda and her family have been fundraising for them yearly in either the BMO Vancouver Marathon or Scotiabank half-marathon runs as Team Heimburger.

Currently, Guelda sits on the Board of Directors for the British Columbia Schizophrenia Society Foundation.

Praying for the best but preparing for the worst, Guelda keeps a watchful eye on her son and realizes just how fragile the human mind can be. Things are good now, but there are never any guarantees. More research is desperately needed.

If you have any questions or concerns regarding severe mental illness, please visit the BCSS website at www.bcss.org

---

ANNA AU

FORGIVENESS

THIS IS A BIG WORD I DON'T UNDERSTAND

As of 2022, Anna Au is 56 years old, living with her partner and her two adult sons in Edmonton, Alberta.

Her whole career in Canada has been involved in the Natural and Organic Food industry. Anna's current job is with a Quebec organic cheese & butter company as their Western Canada

Accounts Manager. She has been given the nickname "The Cheese Lady." 😊

Anna's off-work hours are busy with a variety of activities. She is a certified Zumba instructor and will be getting her certification as a fitness instructor in December 2022. Her passion for Zumba started about ten years ago, and it has been a lifesaver for her, mentally and physically.

Her weekly games of scrabble with her buddy are also one of the highlights of the week.

On the weekend, Anna coaches Special Olympics 5-pin bowling. Her older son is also one of the players.

Friday night is always date night for Anna and her partner. They lost their dog a year ago and now just adopted a kitten into their family. Shelby is a bright boy with tons of character. She is still a cat newbie owner and has been told to be brave and to start with a ginger cat! 😊

Anna appreciates all the positive and wonderful people in her life and thanks God for all she has.

EMILY CRONK

BURN THE CANDLE

AT BOTH ENDS

Emily Cronk is a mother of two and a trained chef, and her trade of choice is drywall.

She is a background actor and, more recently, an author. She volunteers on the PAC for her daughter's school, as well as for community projects in her spare time.

Emily has always had a passion for feeding people good food and making them feel at home.

You can tell being a mother has always been her main path, though, because she is kind, helpful, forgiving, and patient while parenting. She is creating a safe space for her children to feel loved, understood, while breaking generational trauma.

Emily would love to go to school one day to do community outreach and addiction counselling. She hopes that her story will help people feel like there is someone else out there who understands, cares for them and is rooting for them to succeed and achieve their hopes and dreams.

Emily would like to remind people that life is full of such beautiful experiences and moments and if they weren't here, they would missed not only the bad days, but every good day destined for them as well.

NOELLA COTE

A TALE OF A GIRL WHO WAS MADE TO FEEL SHE WASN'T WORTHY

YET SHE STILL FOUND HER WAY

Noella is a Metis women currently living in her home town. Which is located in The Northwest of British Columbia, a 16-hour drive from the Capital. Noella has lived here her whole life, 32 years.

She values her health and wellness, and this has allowed her to become sober. She worked very hard to get herself to that place in her life. She has two girls ages 11 and 10 years old and continued to have two more children with her now husband. Two beautiful sons ages 2 and 3.

Noella is currently working as a licensed Early Childhood Educator! On her down time she enjoys hiking, running, and exploring the surrounding area with her family. She advocates for mental health resources in her community and is the Chairperson on the Parent Advisory Counsel for her daughter's school.

Noella hopes her story will help heal others who have been through a similar experience.

TESSA WHITE

GENERATION TRAUMA

I REFUSE TO BE ANOTHER STATISTIC

Tessa was born in Winnipeg, Manitoba and spent her childhood split between various places in

Manitoba and British Columbia. She currently resides in Alberta with her husband, teenage son, and two well-loved and well-fed cats.

She has always had a passion for writing. Her hobbies include crocheting, trying to avoid the winter, and writing poetry. When she's not working, she is spending time drinking coffee and forgetting to water her many houseplants.

Her favorite authors include Harper Lee, Dean Koontz, and Stephen King. She hopes to encourage others to reach their ambitions and face their fears through her words.

KATHERINE RITCHIE

EMPOWERMENT

COMES WHEN WE LET GO

Kate lives on Vancouver Island in British Columbia.

She gained a bachelor's degree in Social Work and a Master of Arts degree from the University of Victoria, after which she worked in the field of mental health and addictions, and she now works in government policy.

To manage chronic pain, Kate stays active and enjoys hiking, long walks with her family, and trips around the Gulf Islands. Kate plans to continue writing her story and loves to crochet and knit in her free time (when baby is napping, that is).

...

"If someone doesn't care to accept you, respect you, believe in you, don't hesitate to move on and let them go. There are many who love and appreciate you just the way you are."

Amaka Imani Nkosazana

PART 2

WOMEN LIKE ME

"How wonderful! How wonderful!
All things are perfect, exactly as they are."

Buddha

MEET JULIE FAIRHURST

Julie Fairhurst is a Transformational Story Coach and the Founder of the Women Like Me Program.

Julie was a certified prevention educator with the Canadian Red Cross. She has been delivering empowering workshops to adolescents and adults on the issues affecting their safety. She has presented to organizations such as the Vancouver Police Department, Justice Institute, University of British Columbia, and Capilano College. Behavioral Society of British Columbia, Surrey Memorial Hospital. Teachers Association of North Vancouver, and Shine Live, as well as appearing on television and in video.

Julie had a chaotic upbringing and thought her life was set for failure, following down the paths of her previous generations. As a young teenager, she was headed in the wrong direction, and a social worker told her, "There is no hope for you."

But, somewhere deep inside, that young girl inside her showed up and reminded her that she wanted better for her life and the life of her children. Julie had no support from anyone, not a soul. She had to do it all on her own.

Was it an easy road? No, it was far from easy. Julie was a single mom for 24 years. She and her children lived off government handouts. Julie stood in line at food banks to feed her kids. At Christmas, they received Christmas hampers, and she would go to the toy bank to get presents for her children. The path was hard to change, especially when it was all she knew. But she did it.

Julie went back to school and finished her education. She built an outstanding career in sales, marketing, and promotion. She won the company's top awards and was the first woman to achieve top salesperson year after year in a male-dominated industry. She was a sales manager for some of the country's most prestigious developers.

Some people say never to look back, but Julie does every day. Why? Because she never wants to forget the journey that led her to where she is today. And today, her life is entirely different. Julie didn't just fall into this life. She worked at it every day, all the time.

Then, in 2019, Julie's beautiful 24-year-old niece died from a drug overdose on the streets of Vancouver, Canada. And that was the day she said enough! Her niece's death indirectly resulted from the generational beliefs and abuse that some of her siblings continue with their destructive lifestyles.

Julie believes that when we don't deal with our traumas, we pass the dysfunction along to the next generation. This is what happened to her beautiful young niece. This is where her passion comes from, the reason she started Women Like Me.

Everyone can change their story, no matter what their story is right now or what it has been in the past. Everyone's story matters, and that includes yours. And we can rewrite our stories. It's not that hard to do. Reach out if I can help you.

Want to connect with Julie?

Email: julie@changeyourpath.ca

Women Like Me Stories

www.womenlikemestories.com

Find Julie on Social Media:

YouTube – Julie Fairhurst Women Like Me

https://www.youtube.com/
channel/UChFnLgiUC9mWnvp7jikKBw

Women Like Me on Facebook

https://www.facebook.com/StoryCoachJulieFairhurst

Rock Star Strategies on Facebook

https://www.facebook.com/juliefairhurstcoaching

LinkedIn - Julie Fairhurst Women Like Me Stories

https://www.linkedin.com/in/womenlikemestories/

Instagram – Women Like Me Stories

https://www.instagram.com/womenlikemestories/

TikTok

https://www.tiktok.com/@womenlikemestories

...

"Memories are meant to serve you, not enslave you."

A.J. Darkholme

WOMEN LIKE ME COMMUNITY

If you do not belong to Women Like Me Community – Julie Fairhurst, I would be pleased if you decided to join us.

The Women Like Me Community – Julie Fairhurst is a Facebook group of like-minded women. Women who want to pay it forward and lift others to promote healing in the world.

Ages range from 17 to 83 from all over the world and from all walks of life and all over the world.

As a community, we write community books, with the proceeds going to charity. Maybe you will join in on the next book?

Together, as a group, we can help promote healing in our world.

Join the Movement on Facebook:

Come to the community and spend time with other inspiring women. We are waiting for you!

Women Like Me Community – Julie Fairhurst

https://www.facebook.com/groups/879482909307802

...

"I can't explain that, except to say there's release in knowing the truth no matter how anguishing it is. You come finally to the irreducible thing, and there's nothing left to do but pick it up and hold it. Then, at least, you can enter the severe mercy of acceptance."

Sue Monk Kidd

WOMEN LIKE ME BOOK SERIES

Do you have a story that needs to be told? A story that may be holding you back from living your best life. Or, possibly, you have overcome and are ready to share with the world, hoping that your story will invoke another to live a better life.

Writing is therapeutic to the soul. Writing about your past events can be beneficial, both emotionally and physically. You can increase your feelings of well-being and even enhance your immune system.

We only get one chance. Our lives are not a dress rehearsal for our next lifetime. We only get this one life, and it's here and now.

Reach me at www.womelikemestories.com and let me know you are ready to tell your story. The world is waiting for you.

Women Like Me Stories

https://womenlikemestories.com/tell-your-story/

...

"I've always been just me, but I was the last to know that it was all right."

Byron Katie

READ MORE FROM JULIE FAIRHURST

Books are available on Amazon or the Women Like Me Stories website.

Sales and Personal Growth

- Transferring Enthusiasm – The Sales Book For Your Business Growth
- Positivity Makes All The Difference
- Agent Etiquette – 14 Things You Didn't Learn In Real Estate School
- 7 Keys to Success – How to Become A Real Estate Badass
- 30 Days to Real Estate Action – Real Strategies & Real Connections
- Marketing Analysis and Consultation – How To Win Business Over Your Competition

---

Women Like Me Book Series

- Women Like Me – A Celebration of Courage and Triumphs
- Women Like Me – Stories of Resilience and Courage
- Women Like Me – A Tribute to the Brave and Wise
- Women Like Me – Breaking Through the Silence
- Women Like Me – From Loss to Living

Women Like Me Community Book Series

- Women Like Me Community – Messages to My Younger Self
- Women Like Me Community – Sharing Words of Gratitude
- Women Like Me Community – Sharing What We Know to Be True
- Women Like Me Community – Journal for Self-Discovery
- Women Like Me Community – Sharing Life's Important Lessons

www.ingramcontent.com/pod-product-compliance
Lightning Source LLC
Chambersburg PA
CBHW032032040426
42449CB00007B/871

* 9 7 8 1 9 9 0 6 3 9 0 9 8 *